The

Virgin Chronicles

THE VIRGIN CHRONICLES

A Memoir

Marina DelVecchio

SHE WRITES PRESS

Copyright © 2022, Marina DelVecchio

All rights reserved. No part of this publication may be reproduced, distributed, or transmitted in any form or by any means, including photocopying, recording, digital scanning, or other electronic or mechanical methods, without the prior written permission of the publisher, except in the case of brief quotations embodied in critical reviews and certain other noncommercial uses permitted by copyright law. For permission requests, please address She Writes Press.

Published 2022
Printed in the United States of America
Print ISBN: 978-1-64742-337-7
E-ISBN: 978-1-64742-338-4
Library of Congress Control Number: 2021918114

For information, address:
She Writes Press
1569 Solano Ave #546
Berkeley, CA 94707

She Writes Press is a division of SparkPoint Studio, LLC.

Book design by Stacey Aaronson

All company and/or product names may be trade names, logos, trademarks, and/or registered trademarks and are the property of their respective owners.

Names and identifying characteristics have been changed to protect the privacy of certain individuals.

For Joseph and Marina, my two hearts

"But why is it that women have related to and through men? By virtue of having been brought up in a male society, we have internalized the male culture's definition of ourselves. That definition views us as relative beings who exist not for ourselves, but for the servicing, maintenance and comfort of men. That definition consigns us to sexual and family functions, and excludes us from defining and shaping the terms of our lives."

from "The Woman-Identified Woman"

THE VIRGIN WHORE

"*Putana*," my mother, Ann, screams at my retreating back, her head sticking so far out of our third-floor window that I think she might just fall out. *Putana* comes from the Greek word *puta*, which is a vulgar term for the vagina. *Putana* then is one who uses her vagina with depravity. In Italian, it means bitch, and in Indian folklore, *putana* is a demoness who breastfed the infant God Krishna in an attempt to kill him with her poisoned breast milk. In all cultures, *putana* is a derogatory term for women, but in my Greek culture, it is the worst name a woman could be given. A whore.

Mind you, I am twenty-one years old, still a virgin, and headed to my best friend's house two blocks away. It's Friday night, eight o'clock to be exact, and after a week of work and classes for me at Queens College and Pace University for Joyce, we want to unwind. Unwinding on a Friday night means going to Joyce's house, taking off my shoes as soon as I pass through the Chinese threshold of her iron-gated door in our Queens neighborhood, and crashing on her couch. With a blanket draped over us, an array of soda cans and junk food bags piled against each other on the low oak table in front of us, we settle in to watch Disney Princess movies.

What a whorish thing to do, indeed.

We always start with *The Little Mermaid*, because we still believe that it's a love story at its core, not concerned that Ariel's task is to get the guy without using her voice or showing her intelligence; then we settle into *Beauty and the Beast*, because Belle loves books and so do Joyce and I, dreaming of ending up with a boy who will love us enough to save us from the mediocrity of our existence; and finally, we end the night and open the new day with an oldie, *Dumbo* or *Snow White* or *Cinderella*, because we want to have a good cry, laugh at each other through our tears, and get tired enough that we are finally ready to stretch into sleep like cats, extending our limbs until they loosen, forcing us to submit to the weight behind our eyes, bending towards dreams that lie beyond Queens and our sad, boyfriendless lives. Sometimes, I end up falling asleep on her couch until two in the morning.

"Kathy," Joyce shakes me awake. "You gotta go. Your mom's gonna be pissed."

"Yeah," I yawn and slink out from beneath the blanket that smells of her home, her culture, her dad's cooking—soy sauce, ginger, fried fish—the cold air of the room stinging as I move towards the door, put my shoes on, and prepare myself for the meeting with my mom.

I walk slowly, knowing what awaits me when I get to my own house just a few blocks away. It takes me ten minutes to get there, because I am dragging my feet, my shoulders hunched and heavy as they propel me forward against my will.

Using my key to get into the three-story building my mother owns, I slog up to the third floor, past Mr. Thompson's apartment and our laundry room on the main floor, past the second floor where the Isaacs live, an older couple that keeps to themselves until I use too much water in the mornings and they feel the need to tell my mother they were forced to take cold showers—again—and then onward to the third floor, where our apartment starts and ends. My mother owns the entire building, and Paul Thompson and the Isaacs are her tenants. They all keep to themselves, but I think they assume this approach because of my mother. She keeps to herself, and the only time they speak to each other is if there is a plumbing issue or hot water issue or heating issue. Otherwise, it is as if we are all three separate entities that stay out of each other's way. Aside from our respective spaces in the building, we have nothing else in common and no reason to speak to each other.

As soon as the second key on my key ring turns into the lock on our apartment's door, I know I'm in trouble. The door is unlocked, but the padlock, for which I have not been given a key, is secured and I have no way of getting into the apartment. I have to knock on the door for my mother to let me in.

It's after two in the morning at this point, and I don't want to wake up everyone in the building, so I just keep knocking. After the third time, I curl my fingers into a fist and pound on the door. I am so tired, and all I can think of is my small, creaky, twin-sized bed with sagging mattress and all.

Eventually, I hear the echoes of her quiet movements on the other side of the door. I snort when I hear the chain being dragged from the frame to the door. Then the sound of the main lock being turned reaches me, and I can almost see my bed, feel the warmth of the blanket as it closes me in the darkness I wish for. She pulls the door open for me but blocks my entry so that I can't move around her and walk to the left and through the corridor leading to my room.

Because her body is in my way, I am forced to enter to the right, where our formal living room is. I say formal because the only time we sit in this room is when we have company. When I was little, in elementary school, I remember one day bringing my books and notebooks to this room, attempting to do my homework on the carpeted floor, but when she came home from work and saw me lying on my stomach, my head tilted to the side with a pencil in my mouth trying to solve some long division problem, she immediately picked up my things and ushered me out of there.

"This room is used only for company," she told me in no uncertain terms.

And it is. We only sit on the long, low blue-floral plastic-covered couches from the 1950s when we have people over. This isn't often. They come over for Christmas or New Year's; otherwise, my house never bustles with human chatter and laughter. It is mostly quiet, but not the easy quiet you yearn for or find comfort in when you want to escape people and the hurt they bring. It is the uncomfortable kind of quiet—the kind that makes you feel unrooted, detached from yourself and your surroundings. The kind that leaves you hungry for a human face, a smile, a touch, even from someone you don't very much care about. Anyone will do in this kind of quiet that renders me invisible.

The only people who are ever invited into our home are her first cousin, Mike, his wife, Angie, and their son, Nicholas. Her old friend Helen and her husband John is another couple invited, but since Helen's nervous breakdown when I was around thirteen, she has unraveled, lost in memories she recites like poetry, indecipherable and enigmatic phrases that feel loosely attached to reality, barely recognizing anyone except her husband, on whom my mother blames the breakdown. My mother sees her once in a while and talks about her even less, but I have not seen her since that thirteenth summer of my childhood. I am used to people coming in and going out, disappearing with the ease of barely discernible clouds of mist hanging over the water's cool surface.

My mother and I are the only constant stars in our dismantling universe, dimly lit flames against an expansive burst of black and blue canvas barren of life and light. Perhaps this is why no one notices us. No one ever looks for us, not knowing we want to be found, to be seen, by someone. They can't hold on to us long enough to say they want us. At least this is how I feel, and I think my mom, even though she claims she wants to be alone, in the dark and quiet places inside her, feels the same. If she wanted to be alone, she wouldn't have adopted me. She needs the spaces of her life to be filled, and a child can fill those needs without taking away her independence or freedom. This is why I think she adopted me. But there are too many holes, too many hollow caverns that I am too small and weak to fill for her. I'm beginning to find them also in myself.

Even our small apartment, while spacious with two bedrooms, two bathrooms, an office, a kitchen, dining room, and living room all connected by a long, straight hallway seems too big for the two of us. We get lost in all the open spaces. Our days are hushed, the only sounds that reach our ears coming from the rustle of the papers she grades, a cough here or there, voices that reach towards me from the only television set in the house residing in her room. Our thoughts are as silent as our words are, only splintering through the silence when she is angry with me and I lash back and then beg for forgiveness so I can be seen again by her eyes and exist in the physical spaces I occupy. Even my sobs have learned to come out without a sound, my body sagging and writhing in the pain it takes to make myself mute.

On the nights I come home late from Joyce's house, my mother's stocky, sixty-one-year-old body consumes the spaces that lead me to my room, blocking me from the slumber and peace I yearn for, her long, freckled arms motioning me to step to the right and sit on the couch that only our guests can occupy. I take my place in the corner, the slight weight of my body forcing the plastic cover to crease, releasing the swooshing sound of air being compressed. I hug the armrest and sit forward, arming myself, awaiting the inevitable.

She sits opposite me in a matching loveseat, her eyes taking me in, back rigid against the chair, legs crossed in front of her in an elegance I cannot imitate. A cold, aloof elegance. My eyes are lowered, in shame, even though I have not done anything wrong. Except being late. Except being wrong. The wrong girl picked from the anonymous hat full of other little girls she could have adopted.

"Where were you?" Her voice digs into my ribs, forcing my limbs to shrink from its menacing tone.

"I told you. I went to Joyce's." My eyes roll towards her face, clashing with her gaze for a second, long enough to encounter her disapproval of me.

"I don't believe you." She crosses her arms against her bosom and arches her left eyebrow, casting at me a look I have grown used to. I am a liar, she tells me without words. I don't need words to know her thoughts. "Were you drinking?" She spits the words at me.

"No."

She sucks her lips, making the sound of disbelief I cannot defend myself against. "Did you have sex?"

My jaw drops. "With Joyce?" The question comes out in a squeal. I can't wait to tell Joyce this. She is a romantic Chinese girl with protective parents and as innocent as I am. Neither of us has a boyfriend, and our dates are short-lived and without fire. How would sex play out for us? "We were at her house watching Disney movies. We drank Coke and ate cheese-doodles. That's all. You can call her mom. She was there."

The "call her mom" comment is a dig, but she doesn't seem fazed by it. My mother has a habit of interfering with my friendships. When I was eleven, she called Joyce's home and, as Joyce told it to me, demanded she not be my friend. I was using her, my mother told her. Joyce began crying, and her mother took the phone from her to talk to my mom. After she listened to my mother's antics, Mrs. Yung demanded in a thick English accent that she not call her daughter again. Joyce has been afraid of my mother since we met in fourth grade, and this interaction cemented that fear. Even though she lives two blocks from me, we stopped hanging out for the next nine years since we both graduated from sixth grade and moved on to separate middle schools. We never bumped into each other, but I was a straight home-to-school and school-to-home kind of kid with no extracurricular activities so there was never any room for me to hang out. My home was empty of friends and sounds only the living make.

This changed when we started college. She was at Pace University in Manhattan studying finance and I was majoring in literature at Queens College, but somehow, we bumped into each other on the train one day and picked up where we left off.

We were still eleven-year-old girls lurking beneath maturing bodies, innocent, yearning for adulthood and all that came with it, like love and passion and being wanted. But until we felt ready for the responsibilities of going out like young adults and understanding the complexities and pains of relationships, we settled for Friday night couch fests with Disney love stories, learning about love and romance from princesses and princes since our parents did not have these talks with us.

So, when my mother suggests I am out drinking and having sex, it is the funniest thing in the world to me. Funny and sad and so pathetic I want to reach for her, shake her, and slap the smug expression off her freckled face.

I am twenty-one and still a virgin. And I am okay with it. Sex is not on my mind. Love is, and I won't have one without the other. She would know this if she ever asked me, instead of accusing me. But she doesn't ask because she doesn't care about the truth. Not my truth. She has already decided who I am.

I am a whore. A virgin whore.

THE VIRHOUSE

I live in a virgin's home.

"I think my mother's a virgin," I tell Joyce one Friday night in between films.

"What makes you say that?" Joyce asks with doubt eased into the lines on her forehead. She is one of the few friends I have who knows I am adopted. My adoption, which took place when I was eight years old, is a secret I am not allowed to share with anyone, and when my mother discovers that I have told someone, even Joyce, she exposes me to a pained expression that makes me feel like I have just stabbed her in the stomach, twisting the knife in, gutting her and leaving her open for ridicule. She wants us to pretend that I was born out of her womb, that I traveled through the bloody cavity of her entrails and was handed to her by a set of bloodied hands belonging to ghostly nurses. She doesn't tell me this, but I know it. I know it the way I know I will be met with an irredeemable silence that she will cloak herself with after the truth slips from my lips, as if I am cheating on her, pretending that I don't exist, her body passing me in the hallway or on the stairs leading to the apartment we share, her head cocked in the opposite direction, her lips taut and severe, wordlessly expressing the affront of my existence.

"To have sex, you have to be open, intimate. You have to like men. And she hates men."

"I doubt it." Joyce crinkles her nose.

"Think about it." I sit up straight and face her, placing a teal blue pillow on my lap to rest my fidgety hands on. "In all the years I have lived with her, she has never dated. Not once brought a man home or gone out with one."

"Maybe she goes on dates and you don't know about them."

"Nah. I'm always with her. Not when she's at work. But think about it. My entire childhood, I have gone wherever she has gone. She travels with me, she goes out to the movies and dinner with me. Everything is with me. When she went to night school, I waited for her in the library or outside her class. There have been no men. In all her stories, there are no men. She thinks making out is disgusting, blow jobs are repulsive, and she laughs at men all the time."

"Maybe she likes women," Joyce giggles.

"Yah, I don't think so."

And then we laugh, our snickers only waning when the Disney logo and music fill the spaces of our wanting hearts, living vicariously through animated beauties awaiting their prince charmings and first kisses. Kisses like the one I shared with Danny in high school and have been pining for ever since, kissing boys just to see if they could trigger that sensation of being suspended on a cloud of hope and swirliness overtaking my body, weakening beneath the softness of his lips, the sweet taste of his tongue inside my mouth. But I have yet to find a boy whose kiss has matched Danny's. And I have kissed a good number of boys since high school.

Danny is also the first boy I ever brought into my home, the home that never opens its doors to the male species unless they are plumbers or my mother's cousin Mike and his son Nicholas. My mother is at work, and I just finished my last year of high school. Danny knows I love him. I tell him one night when I am drunk in his house, downing straight vodka as if it is the courage I need to say the words to him.

"Kathy, I love you, too," he sighs. "But I can't. I have a girlfriend. You know this."

Choose me, I want to whisper against his lips, to crush my chest into his, shove my love in his face so he has to choose me. But I stand the few feet away from him that he puts between us, brimming with liquor and desire I find so difficult to contain in my small frame. I want to throw up both, their toxicity poisoning my insides.

Helen. Yes, I know her name. I also know that if we are both drowning, he won't be able to choose which one to save, because he loves us both. These are his words while he waits with me for my mother to pick me up from the party he hosts for all of us graduating in a few weeks and going off to different colleges and paths that will never merge again. At least, not for me.

"Come to my house next week." I look up at him, my eyes wavering and sullen with drunkenness. "I want you to see where I live. I'm probably never going to see you again. Just as friends."

He pauses, his long, tapered fingers reaching out to steady me when I loosen my gaze from his and I lose my balance. "Okay," he says quietly.

"Promise," I demand.

"I promise," he whispers against my hair, pausing long enough to plant a kiss against my cheek. I don't want a cheek kiss. I want more. All of me vibrates with the want of more.

When my mom picks me up, I watch from my blurry vision as the road we travel on increases the distance between me and his own retreating back.

"What were you doing at his house?" my mother asks me once I rest my head against the seat holding me still. The only part of me wobbling is my head when the wheels of my mother's green Chevy hits an unexpected pothole or sails over the grainy and uneven terrain of the highway leading us to our home in Elmhurst.

"Nothing," I mumble. "We just hung out and talked."

"His parents were home?" she confirms.

"Yes. They checked in on us, but they mostly stayed upstairs," I explain, placing my fingers against my temple to ease the pain that has begun to unfold and pound behind my eyes. I want her to stop asking me questions, and I release a sound of exasperation, turning my face away from her.

There is a long pause.

"Let me smell your breath." Her voice is icy, but I obey, turning my head to her and breathing into her face with exaggerated force, her eyes locking with my unstable ones for the second she takes hers off the road.

"You were drinking," she accuses me, and before I know it, I feel the burning sting of her palm against my cheek. My mother doesn't hit me often, but the few times she has, I feel an ache inside me that cries out for more. Whether it is a slap or a caress, I ache for human touch—and not just anyone's touch, but hers. I want to feel skin and fingers prying hair away from my face or a tender caress or the feel of her body enveloping mine, not turning away from me. With touch comes love, the knowledge that you're present, that you exist. That you are loved.

I hold back the tears stinging my eyes by thinking of Danny. We've been friends for the past year. I see him in the halls and in classes we share, but he and I never speak, not until the incident with Frangas occurs. Danny is the grungy boy, dressed in combat boots and black and gray T-shirts and jeans that match his eyes and hair, layers and layers of dark depths that emit no light. He sneaks out of the bathroom window to smoke with other dark-clad boys and girls who don't take school seriously. I am an all-A-student, even in math, a subject that perturbs me to no end. I graduate second in my class, with a 97 average, and never consider cutting classes or behaving in any manner that will tarnish my goody-two-shoes reputation with my teachers and classmates. Danny and I exist in different circles, and the two never intersect—until the day they do.

It is lunchtime during my junior year in high school, and Andrew, our social studies teacher's son, turns to me suddenly, laughing. A bunch of us are standing in a circle talking about something I don't quite recall. His eyes take me in, and with a smirk, he names my secret.

"What do you know? You're a bastard!"

Since I don't talk about my adoption, all my peers know is that I have no father. I only have my mother. Because it is the 1980s and Greek families don't tend to divorce, it is assumed that my mother had me out of wedlock. That I am a bastard. My mother, a whore.

"Fuck you!" I scream at him, and before I know it, my hands spring up to his chest and shove him so hard that he loses his balance and falls off the corner of the desk and flat on his ass. It takes everything I have not to kick him in the face.

I turn away from the crowd and speed towards the school

exit, finding myself outside in the middle of the winter, wearing nothing more than my short-sleeved white shirt and blue-checkered skirt—our Greek school uniform. Once the crisp air strikes my cheeks, I realize how much I hate being cold, but I am too humiliated and angry to go back inside. Hugging my chest, I follow a path away from the school, walking briskly to warm myself and lose the rage that is brimming inside my core.

"Kathy, wait up!" I hear my name being called and turn around. It is Danny, trotting towards me. Confusion settles into skin wrinkles on my forehead. Aside from a few "hey there's" and "yo's" in the hallways, he and I never speak to each other.

"I'm not going back in there," I yell, waiting for him to catch up to me.

"I know. I just want to walk with you," he breathes into the cold air, shortening the distance between us with his long legs.

"Um, why?" I squint at him. He's about five inches taller than my five-foot-one frame. I have to look up to meet his gaze, surprised by the gold flecks I find there, hiding behind the black orbs I have only seen from a distance.

"I heard what Frangas said to you," he starts, referring to Andrew by his last name, "and I was glad you pushed him to the floor. He deserved it."

"I'm not a bastard," I say to him, the words choking in my throat.

"It doesn't matter," Danny points out. "He was out of line."

I stop suddenly, forcing him to freeze in his tracks. "Why do you care? It's not like we're friends." I don't expect my words to come out mean, but they sound mean to me. I only want to be honest. I hate being confused, not knowing people's intentions. Why is he here? Why does he care?

"I want to be your friend." His voice is soft, and it warms me despite the freezing air attacking my senses, watering my eyes and reddening my nose. "And anyway," he adds. "I understand what it's like not to have a father around. My mom's the one raising me."

We walk in silence for a few seconds.

"Are your parents divorced?" I ask.

"Yeah. They divorced when I was eleven. I don't see much of him anymore. He has a whole new family, so it's just me and my mom."

A small tremor runs along my spine, and before I know it, he takes off his leather jacket and puts it around my shoulders.

"You're going to get sick." He smiles at me, and I feel my limbs loosen, my anger slipping off me like water trickling down my skin, smooth and soft, after a long, hot shower.

"I have a father," I tell him without looking at him. "I was adopted by my mom, but before her, I had a mother and a father and brothers and sisters. I just don't talk about them." I don't tell him that the last time I told a small boy at a camping site about my adoption, about the parents and siblings I have, living in Greece, the news of my indiscretion traveled to my mother's ears, and I had to watch as she rushed me to our cabin, packed our things, and drove us out of the campsite in the middle of the night, as if I had just committed an unthinkable crime we had to flee from. I was crouched in my seat in the front of the car, hoping she would talk to me, yell at me, something. But she didn't say a word during the long drive from Pennsylvania to Queens, and after that, she ignored me for a week, shuffling her eyes and her limbs away from me, as if by looking at me, she would be naming our secret, our disgrace. My adoption. I don't tell anyone again that I am adopted. I let them assume my father died. Or left us. That Ann is my only mother, forty years my senior, gray-haired and wrinkled, making all the decisions for both of us.

"Well, you could if you want to. To me. I just want you to know that I understand. You're not alone. Okay?" He stops to look at me, forcing me to halt my own quickened gait.

"Okay." I smile up at him.

"You ready to go back in? You're starting to look like an icicle." He laughs aloud, the sound of it like honey, rich and thick, sliding down my throat.

"I guess. But keep Andrew away from me. If I see him, I'm going to punch his teeth in."

He laughs at that, too, probably because Andrew is almost six feet tall and weighs about two hundred pounds to my meager ninety-five.

After that, Danny and I become fast friends. We have lunch together in school, we walk around the block when we don't bring enough money for lunch, and he reaches out to hug me when he sees me in between classes that we don't share. We never hang out after school, because neither of us has a car and our private lives don't mix. Mine is filled with girls: Alex, Spira, and Rosa. I go to the movies with them, meet them at the mall, or hang out at their house, a few blocks from our high school in Jamaica. I don't hang out with boys, not even Danny.

He introduces me to his friend Ace once. It is half-a-day at school, and he wants me to meet Ace because he thinks we will get along. Ace is sixteen, goes to a public school in Flushing, and comes all the way to Jamaica to hang out with me and Danny and his girlfriend, Helen. I guess it is a double date. Danny winks at me at the end of our lunch date, high-fiving Ace and waving goodbye to me as he walks in the opposite direction with his arm around Helen, a petite girl with black hair and eyes that match Danny's. She's pretty, and I feel that something is missing in my life when he bends to her for a kiss and she receives him with a smile and light in her eyes. Something dark and beautiful. Something like love, which I have only known through books and movies.

Ace is my first kiss. My first French kiss. I have kissed boys before, on the cheek or a rushed peck on the lips, maybe three or four times in my sixteen years. But when Ace touches his lips to mine by the entrance of the subway station in Jamaica that will take me to my home in Elmhurst, I don't expect his tongue to glide across my own lips, part them, and then slide into my mouth. His tongue is soft and gentle as it plays with mine, coaxing it to flex and stretch into his own mouth, to savor the cigarette aftertaste that still clings to his tongue and teeth, and I like it. I like the sensation of exploring the dark, cavernous expanse of his mouth with my tongue, feeling, tasting, relishing the insides of another human being with my eyes closed, which only heightens the experience, our hands compounding the experience by busily touching each other's hair, tugging at the loose strands that deepen the kiss, Ace's fingertips at my throat, my collar bone, the contact of his hands on my waist, pulling me to him, his tongue inside me sending an array of shivers along the surface of my skin, my knees weakening my stance so that I lean into his body for relief, for sustenance, for something solid to hold me up.

When we come up for air, we don't notice strangers staring at us as they wind around us to go down into the black mouth of the subway station. Ace grabs my wrist, pulls a pen out of his black leather jacket, and smiles at me as he writes his phone number on the palm of my hand. He bends over and kisses it, then reaches down and kisses my lips, still red and puffy from the onslaught of his mouth.

"Call me," he says, pressing up against me and forcing a sigh out of my still parted lips.

"Okay," I smile, but as I turn away from him and retreat down the stairs into the cold caverns of the station, running to catch my train home, I already know I won't call him.

That kiss is the most intense kiss I have had, and I know what will come next—what he will come to expect. At sixteen, I am not ready for sex. I only want the kiss, and after that afternoon, I know Ace will not settle for anything less. He will not only want a repeat of what we just shared, but he will also want more. And I don't. My body does, perhaps, but my body does not speak for me. I speak for her.

The following week, Danny comes up to me and asks why I haven't called Ace.

"He really likes you," he nudges me in the ribs. "He's a good guy."

"I know," I tell him, taking books out of my locker and tossing them into my school bag. "I just can't. You know I'm not allowed to date until I'm eighteen. I'm not breaking that rule. My mom would kill me."

"You're hiding," he looks at me knowingly, but grins, tousling my loose brown hair with his long, tanned fingers. Greek and Italian, Danny has the all-year-long brown shade of skin that never fades, even in the dead of winter when the sun fails to evade the ferocity of the gray clouds that make our city look drab and colorless.

"Perhaps," I smile back. "But I'm okay with that. See you tomorrow," I sing, swinging my backpack over my shoulders and rushing out of the range of his intense gaze.

It isn't until the end of senior year that my feelings begin to change for Danny. The mere sight of him makes me uncomfortable in my own skin, wondering if he can see the tremors his one glance births within my body, the pores protruding from my skin when he touches my shoulder or glides his fingers through my hair when we find ourselves talking by our lockers. I grow quiet around him because words like "I love you" or "Kiss me" want to rush out at him through my lips like impatient seagulls rushing toward fingers offering them scraps of food at the beach, the rays of the summer sun beating against the incessant flapping of their unfurled wings.

I think he knows how I feel because my eyes lower when he looks into them for too long. Because my hands rush to my lap when he touches them with his own calloused fingers. Because when I stand before him drunk and stupid, I beg him to come to my house, as friends, when everything in my body screams for more. I don't want to have sex with him. I know this as much as I know nothing will happen between us. But I need to have him near me the way you need oxygen to breathe—the way you need the touch of someone you trust and love to know that you exist.

Three days after our high school graduation, Danny takes a train from his Flushing to my Elmhurst. He is the first boy to enter the austere threshold of my mother's home, and it feels like a symbolic awakening, my rebirth from a girl into a young woman. I am breaking my mother's rules, slipping into the wanton threads of the whore, willingly, intentionally. Bludgeoning the harlot-laden labels with which my mother corrodes my girlhood, my sexual identity, I do so with the intensity needed to define my own sexuality—whether it is to be virginal, whorish, or something sane and palatable in between.

Danny is shy around me, quietly following me on the short tour I give him of our apartment: the kitchen where I offer him water, the dining room and living room that only see company during the holidays, my mother's room that will eventually be shut with a lock to keep me out of her things and away from her phone, and then into my room, which I share with my tabby cat, Treasure. We sit on the edge of my bed, and I unfold my photo albums onto our laps, our knees touching, mine trembling a little bit at the feel of his dark hair brushing against my shaved legs. We are both wearing shorts and T-shirts, and beads of sweat trickle down our necks. Late in June, it is hot in my apartment, and the only air conditioner is attached to our living room window, on the opposite side of the apartment. Eventually, we both lean back against my slack pillow, lying side by side, and my head is filled with this fuzziness that feels like more pleasure than pain. It is a sweet aching that wants to be fed and caressed at the same time. My skin prickles with sensation, and my flesh is feverish and in agony, gravitating towards his long limbs for any kind of contact, hungering for a touch, a long-awaited taste of him.

"Will you kiss me already?" I whisper heavily into his neck and then find myself crushed beneath the slight weight of his lithe body, our arms clasping each other with the fear of letting go. Our lips meet and open, our tongues feeling at home in each other's mouths, knowing the love that lives inside, patiently abiding—a lover's welcome.

We kiss like this for an hour. Our hunger, once nourished,

eventually subsides into a more gentle and inquisitive exploration. Our kissing is intimate, deep, lustful, but he doesn't taint it by trying for more. He knows I am a virgin. I know he isn't. And while his fingers trail up and down the skin of my throat, my arms, the outline of my curved hips, they don't go anywhere else, anywhere private or hidden by my clothes. I feel safe with him, able to lose myself in our kiss without overthinking what I will do if he wants to unhook my bra or press his genitals into mine. Kissing me is enough for him, and his choices never force me to think of mine. This makes me love him even more. When we finally pull away, we lie into each other, his arms holding me to his lean chest, my ear listening to the heavy thudding of his heart, our bare legs intertwined.

As I walk him to the subway station before my mother gets home from work, he pulls me into a hug and bends over to kiss me. It is our last kiss. It is the last time I will ever see him.

DRINKING  LIKE A VIRGIN

I've kissed lots of boys since Danny, but I haven't loved any of them. These boys are not my friends. They're just boys I meet at parties or at clubs. And our kisses, while passionate and intense, never make me want to do more or go further than our bodies pressed against the driver's side of their cars where I plant a final kiss on their beer-laced lips and walk away from them, not caring if they call or not. I don't call them. They'll eventually want more, and I don't. Kissing is enough for me. For now. I choose my virginity. Maybe I am more like my adoptive mother than I think. Rigid. Withholding. Cold.

"I don't need a man to feel complete," she often tells me when I am getting ready to go out on a date or dancing.

"You're saying that I do?" I query, already feeling the blood rush to my cheeks, going to that heady and blind place that makes me want to lash out physically. I want to punch her. It takes so much not to. I am waiting for the usual insult. Whore. That's what I am because I go out on dates, or to parties, or to Joyce's house to watch Disney movies.

"Well," she looks at me pointedly and says no more. It's all in her face—the smirk outlining the thin lips I have learned to loathe, her small, beady brown eyes that run their gaze up and down my slim body, clothed in tight jeans, a onesie tank top that snaps at the crotch, a red-and-black checkered flannel shirt tied at my waistline, and combat boots that make me feel tough, strong, aggressive. Like I occupy space. All the things I am not. This is my Saturday outfit, and after I apply a dark brown shade of lipstick on my own thin lips, I am ready to go dancing with Joyce and Helen, my drinking and dancing friends.

I don't always drink. I am eighteen during my first stint with alcohol, and it only leaves me depressed. I attend parties at my friends' homes and sip their drinks, not wanting to commit to one of my own, not sure which drink to ask for. There is beer, mostly. Some gin and tonic, some Coke and rum lined on the kitchen table, and I move along the length of it, sipping from each cup to find my own special flavor—the one I will spend the rest of my adult life requesting at bars with confidence—but this doesn't happen. What does happen is me, getting too drunk on all the mixed drinks and feeling my body slide down the wall that keeps me stationary, until my butt finds the floor, and then staying there in stupor, weeping like a child for a mother who doesn't see her, doesn't love her in the way she needs.

"Kathy, it'll be okay." My friends take turns patting my back, giving me tissues to blow my nose with, stroking me with this piteous gaze that makes me feel smaller than I want to feel. After three similar events that always end with me crying, on the floor, unable to stop, unable to articulate my pain, I stop cold. I still go to parties. I still hang out with my college friends, but I don't drink. I am too ashamed. I have become the unhinged pain-in-the-ass friend that everyone must abandon a good time to take care of, and I don't want to be that friend. The messy one. The tiresome one. I would lose patience with someone like that, and

I like my friends too much to lose them over my emotional tur-moil. So, no more pity for me. No more public displays of aching needs not being met. No more drinking.

But now I'm legal. Twenty-one. And I have more control over my emotions, or at least I know how to hide them better. At twenty-one, I have found my place next to Joyce again, this time not as the eleven-year-old girl with whom I rode my bike and who copied my math homework but as a young woman with a slew of friends who spend the weekends going to clubs or bars and drinking. In my twenties, this is new to me.

The first time I pop my drinking cherry for real, Joyce has invited me to one of her friends' parties. They are all from col-lege and I don't know any of them, but there is alcohol every-where and no parents in sight. One cup of something strong in my system, and I find myself being ushered into a bed with Joyce placing a wastebasket in front of my mouth so I can vomit into it. And I do. Quite a few times.

"I'm a virgin!" I yell into the room of girls tending to me.

"A virgin ho!" A faceless boy's voice yells back from another room.

I toss my insides into the can, and Joyce leads my head back onto the pillow, giving me tissues with which to wipe my sour mouth. She is such a good caregiver. A good friend.

"Are you alright?" Mike's voice reaches for me in the dark. I am unable to see his brown eyes or his muscular build until he stands an inch away from me, his hand clasping mine on the bed. Up until twenty minutes ago, he and I had been talking, when I was still straight and sober, sipping whatever concoction the other kids had put in the bowl I scooped into my red plastic cup. I excused myself to go to the bathroom but never made it back to him. I think the virgin talk is a siren call for boys because he finds me and doesn't leave my side for the rest of the night. Or maybe a drunk girl always spells "easy." No fight. No resistance.

"I'm good." I cough, my body convulsing again. Joyce thrusts the can in front of me and holds it there as I throw up into it again. I scrunch my nose at her wry smile, glad she is with me. I think she feels guilty because this is the first party she has brought me to, and I'm so drunk I can't even stand on my own two feet. She feels responsible.

Mike reaches over and wipes a tendril of my brown hair away from my wet chin. He leans over and kisses me. His tongue runs over my lips until they part and threads its way into my mouth. As drunk as I am, I can feel Joyce's fingers twisting into my arm. She and I are thinking the same thing: how gross this guy is, kissing me right after I throw up, dregs of it still on my teeth, tongue, and insides. A headache begins to find root behind my glazed eyes, and I can't help but wonder if I am going to throw up again, this time in his mouth. Any future between Mike and me is over right there and then, when he leans into me and kisses my vomit-ridden mouth. What other crazy shit will he be into if this doesn't deter him from pursuing me? I don't want to know.

After that, I start going to clubs with Joyce and her friends. Our drinks consist of sharing a bottle of flavored Snapple tea with vodka poured into it in the parking lots of the clubs we frequent, hiding it in Helen's bag and then meeting in a bathroom stall, the three of us taking sips from it throughout the night. I don't need to drink to enjoy myself, and most nights the music I dance to is more intoxicating than the actual alcohol I consume. When the novelty of Snapple and vodka wears off, I find myself on the dance floor, moving rhythmically to the music, by myself. It's the one place I don't feel alone, even if my friends are nowhere to be found.

My favorite club is Malibu's in Long Island. It has two dance floors, and I spend hours on each one, making different friends, moving to different types of music. The main one—with the biggest dance floor—only plays new wave music; the second one plays club music. Whatever you are in the mood for, each floor can provide it. I don't really care which songs are playing. On any dance floor, I can close my eyes and feel the notes, the drumbeat, the bass as it skips along the length of my arms and legs, up to my torso, through me and into me, like a lover with knowing hands. It is easy to surrender to the music, my limbs shimmying and swaying to chords that whisper along my skin, a slow, languid caress that guides me from one side of the floor to the other without force, vibrating from my toes to the scalp on my head. It is a safe surrender, an easy kind of love, and I give myself to the music without hesitation or regret, without alcohol in my system, my thoughts serene, my mother's voice and abhorrent words absent, their force powerless. When I am dancing, she doesn't even exist. It's better than alcohol, better than curling myself into a pitiful ball of shame and regret on the linoleum floor of someone's kitchen, feeling like shit.

That is until I get home, the roar and rumble of Helen's Acura Integra and its faulty muffler fading away after she lets me out of her car at two in the morning. The scene is the same each Saturday night upon my arrival from one club or another.

I let myself into the apartment building, climb the two floors to my apartment's door, turn the key into the lock, and push the door only to encounter its begrudging resistance. I knock on the wooden structure, bang on it with my fists when nothing stirs, and then hear my mother's fingers unlock the deadbolt from the other side. She opens the door with the chain still in place.

"Yes," my mother peers at me through the crack coldly.

"Will you please let me in?" I heave a sigh of frustration. What is the purpose of the chain? Really. What is the reason for any of this, other than to shame me?

"When you come home this late," she begins, "I can't go to sleep. I wait up for you."

"Well, you can go to sleep," I retort. "If you don't lock the doors to the apartment, I can come in on my own and not wake you up."

"I like to know when you get home," she says, sliding the chain back and pulling the door slightly so that I can enter.

"That's your choice," I tell her, yawning. I move to the right, away from her unapproachable form, and sit on the couch, mute. I know the drill. These are the consequences of going out with my friends. For going out at all and returning late. She sits opposite me and her eyes take me in, from head to toe, without uttering a word. There is always the shame, the interrogation of my body, my pupils, for evidence that I am what she has deemed me to be.

A drunk. A druggie. A whore.

Ann sees what she wants to see except what is in front of her. A girl desperate for her mother to see her—the real her. A girl who only drinks occasionally, eventually finding her drink, a white Russian, a concoction of milk and Kahlua that she never finishes, abandoning it half empty as soon as her chin goes numb, her insides feel unfastened, and her mind is free of Ann.

A girl who mostly stops at kissing because when she does allow fingers to unhook her bra and touch her breasts, she ends up crying in the shower, scrubbing the lingering memory of desire off her flesh with soap, vowing never to give in again to boys whose lips feel so warm and inviting against her neck, their hands promising love, always wanting, demanding, taking, pushing, pressing for more than she is able to give.

She is invisible. And her needs don't matter.

THE VIRGIN LEI

The summer of my eighteenth birthday, my mother takes me to Hawaii. It is a gift for graduating from high school and for graduating second in my class. Perhaps the proudest moment she experiences is sitting in the audience, watching me give my salutatorian speech. I am second in my class. I am something, receiving award after award for each one of my academic subjects. I know I have made her proud that day, and I don't expect a gift from her, but a trip to Honolulu is one I will never forget or say no to.

To be clear, Ann is an avid traveler. The inside joke about teachers in New York is that they teach for the summers, stashing their money away during the year to travel in July and August. My mother is a spendthrift, often purchasing my clothes, shoes, and toys at second-hand stores in Long Island and Queens, but when it comes to traveling, her pockets know no limits. The earliest stamps on my passport, between my ninth and fourteenth birthdays, come from airports in Guatemala, Peru, Bolivia, Ecuador—including a two-week ride on a boat that takes us to all the Galapagos Islands, inhabited only by iguanas, turtles, and birds—England and Greece. In between these big trips, we also have smaller ones that take us throughout the United States: Virginia, Washington, New Mexico, California, Pennsylvania, Colorado, Salt Lake City, and so on. We ski in the winter and travel in the summer, but Hawaii has to be my favorite trip because, for the first time, my mother unexpectedly loosens her grip from the invisible but taut umbilical cord that connects us.

It is at the poolside of our hotel on the Honolulu strip that I meet Ray. He is tall, golden-skinned, has a full head of wavy dark-blond hair with red strands that glisten in the sun and stark blue eyes that feel like they are pulling me into him whenever he looks right at me. At first, he is a sun god that I steal glances at when he strides past my lounging chair as I sun myself, not thinking twice about liking him or being given the chance to like him. He is beyond my reach, above my potential in looks. I am small, barely five foot one, with brown shoulder-length hair, limp and stringy, my brown eyes big and wide against my angular face, but nothing extraordinary to look at between my high cheekbones. I am not his type, at least that's what I tell myself when I first see him, longing for a guy like that to give me the time of day.

At eighteen, I don't dress up or do my hair or my nails, the latter of which are bitten down to the nail bed. I don't spend my hard-earned money from my job as a library page on clothes. I'm comfortable in jeans and sneakers, or in very hot climates, like the one born to Hawaii, in shorts, T-shirts, and sneakers. Fixing myself up in makeup makes me feel inauthentic, fake, and so I encounter each day with my real face, not hidden behind rouge or lipstick or cover-up to hide the pimples on my skin. If a boy is going to like me, he is going to like my real face, the real me, not a fake version of me. And other than Danny, whose kiss is a playful shadow still haunting my lips from six weeks earlier, I don't expect to meet any guys, to like any of them. I especially don't think I am going to meet one in Hawaii.

Lazily stretching on the lounger, I pry my sticky legs and thighs off its white plastic strips and pull my long T-shirt over my green one-piece bathing suit. It comes down over my butt and cascades against my thighs in the front. I take a few steps towards the pool and then jump in, welcoming the cool feel of water washing off the heat my thin limbs have sustained from the sun and oil and grime that have stuck to me from the lotion I applied. I am already a shade of dark brown, a gift from my Greek heritage, and I have only sunbathed twice in the five days we have been here. After a while, I walk up to the pool steps, climb them, and make my way to the hot tub a few feet away. Two girls in their twenties are already in there. They are both thin, manicured, pretty, and wearing two-piece suits. I envy the ease with which they navigate their bodies, unashamed of their sun-kissed skin and curves moving languidly against the water's surface.

"Hi," one pipes up.

"Hey," I respond and smile, feeling shy and out of place in my T-shirt that reads "Honolulu, 1989."

I sit opposite them, fold my body into the manufactured bench beneath the gurgling water, lean my head back on the cemented frame, and close my eyes against the sun. I love the feel of its rays against my face. Its intensity does something queer to my entire body. I can feel it responding to the heat, my skin arching into its warmth, butterflies tingling and moving against the insides of my abdomen as if trying to escape their dark confinement.

"Hi, there." A different voice breaks into the sensations

overwhelming my thoughts and body. It is a low voice, thick, and friendly. I try to escape back into my head. I don't want to talk. This is the quietest part of my day, my time without my mother, and I have to hold on to all the energy I will need to be carefree around her when it comes time for dinner, and then later, playing cards on the bed we share in our hotel room. It takes a lot of effort on my part to smile and talk to her as if we are a happy little family of two, to fill the silences between us heavy with old wrongs and burdened with unarticulated defensiveness. I never know what to say to her, and finding words that will keep the conversation light and without depth does not come easy for me. I often want to scream, to beat my fists against something hard, because words seem ineffective, rendering me powerless.

"I'm Ray," the voice interjects again.

The girls giggle their names, and I smile inside, awaiting the hook-up about to take place.

"What about you?" His words pull me out of myself.

"Me?" I open one eye to find him, and then I see the boy whose form I have already memorized, watching him quietly for the past couple of hours behind the dark shades of my sunglasses. Had he noticed me watching him? Suddenly, I want to jump up, slide my way past them, and escape the three sets of eyes that peer at me, waiting for my reply.

"Oh—Kathy," I say, smiling tightly at each of them in return.

"Yeah, I saw you hanging out with my little sister the other day." He flashes me a smile with straight white teeth.

My limbs loosen a bit. "Lillie's your sister?" A very friendly little girl around the age of eleven, Lillie found me in the pool a day earlier and struck up a conversation with me. She was bright and sweet, and I enjoyed spending my free time with her. I met her mother, Lorraine, and they had mentioned Ray, but I had not made the connection. Until now.

"Yeah," he nods his head. "She thinks you're cool."

"Ha!" I snort. "That's funny. She's the cool one. Very mature for her age."

"I agree," he looks away for a minute and then his eyes come back for me. "So, where are you from?" he asks, inching closer to me until he is sitting beside me, his movements disturbing the burst of bubbles erupting from the center of the tub.

"New York."

"Me, too. Where in New York?"

"Queens. Elmhurst," I elaborate since Queens is huge. "You?"

"Brooklyn. That's so cool."

"Small world." My brain is already rummaging through a bag of small talk items I will need to continue this conversation. I am still shocked that he has gravitated to me in this hot tub when there are two pretty girls in the same body of water he could be talking to. If I had any guts, I would ask him, too, but how do you ask a stranger why he chooses to talk to the timid dark-haired girl with a shirt covering her body instead of the pretty, scantily clad ones?

I look over at the girls, who are smiling now, and one of them winks at me.

"We'll see you guys later," she says, giggling, and they glide through the water to the stairs of the hot tub. Exiting and casually walking to where their things are, their tanned shoulders bumping into each other as they whisper and giggle some more.

"Bye," I say, my nails digging into the palm of my hands with nervousness, and I wish they would come back.

When I turn my attention back to Ray, I find his eyes on me. Lightheaded, I try to concentrate on the words that come out of his mouth and not on his actual mouth, wondering what he would taste like—not thinking I would even be given the chance to find out.

"I think Lillie said you were leaving tomorrow," he begins.

"Yes, in the afternoon. What about you?"

"We leave in two days. Back to Brooklyn and the real world."

"Yeah, it has been nice, doing nothing, enjoying the sun and beach. I'm so relaxed here."

"Do you want to hang out tonight?" His question is sudden and takes me by surprise.

"Um, sure," I say, quickly adding, "I have to check with my mom though."

"Oh, no! I get it. I am twenty and a stranger. Let me know after you talk to her. My room number is 203. And she can talk to my mom, also, if she has any questions."

"Okay," I mutter, dumbstruck that this guy—this good looking and older guy—wants to hang out with me. With me.

"Wanna move to the pool and talk some more?"

"Sure." I wait for him to move first and follow him to the stairs of the pool, the cool water sending a shiver down my spine. Or maybe it is Ray's hand on my back as he guides me to the pool's edge. We spend the rest of the afternoon talking, laughing, diving under the surface of the pool water when it gets too hot and then finding our place on the steps again, drawn back to another seamless conversation about home and school. At five o'clock, we separate, going to our rooms to get ready. I still have to ask my mom if I can go out with him. And I'm not sure how that conversation will go, but it has been on my mind the entire time.

"I'll see you by the hotel's entrance in an hour. If you can't make it, just call me at 203. Okay?" He bends over to kiss me on the cheek, and I know that there is nothing that will stop me from seeing him in an hour. Making my way to the elevator, I cross my fingers.

As soon as I enter our room, I find my mother lying down on the queen-sized bed we share. She only occupies the right side of the bed, leaving the other half for my own smaller body.

"Ma," I begin, fidgeting with the hem of my white shirt as it touches the dark skin of my thighs. "This boy, Ray, asked me out tonight. I just spent the day talking to him by the pool, but we met his mom and sister the other day. Remember? Lorraine?"

"Yes. That's fine. What time will you be back?"

I gulp back my surprise. Everyone is acting strangely today. A good-looking guy passes over two beauties for me, and now my mother is letting me go out with a guy I just met. In Hawaii.

Her reaction reminds me of another time that she acted uncharacteristically. During my sophomore year in high school, she had taken me to Greece. On the plane ride, a woman had been sitting with us and spent the entire flight talking to me. She invited us to her beach house in Athens, and my mother took us for a day's visit. The lady had a son my age whose name I don't remember, and he tried talking to me a few times, but I brushed him off. Well, maybe not brushed him off exactly. I was too shy to talk to boys, or at least, stranger-boys I didn't spend the days with in school. The school boys made me feel comfortable because I knew not to take them seriously. They were silly boys that I didn't like or care about. So, when this boy comes to me while I'm sunbathing by the water and asks me a few questions, I answer in monosyllables, not thinking he is trying to hit on me or get to know me. I'm not thinking anything, really, except how odd it is that my mother has accepted an invitation to visit a stranger we just met on the plane. It just isn't like her. Or maybe it is. Maybe I don't know her as well as I think I do. She is a mystery to me, and I don't have the skills needed to unravel her layers. We are strangers to each other, and every conversation we have is like having a conversation with a foreigner who doesn't speak my language.

Upon our return home from vacation, I ask her about it.

"She seemed like a nice lady. She was quite taken with you, so I thought it would be nice to visit her. I really think she wanted you to meet her son. Maybe set you up."

"And you were okay with that?" I gawk at her.

"I didn't see any harm in it. He lives in Greece. You live here. And his mother seemed really nice."

"Were you planning on an arranged marriage or something?"

"Don't be silly, Kathryn," she turns her amber eyes on me, chastising me for my off-handed remark.

Because I want to go out with Ray, I don't press the issue or ask her why she is okay with me going out with a boy I just met at our hotel and an older one at that. I don't care about her reasons, glad to be given this inch of freedom. Maybe she is as tired of my company as I have grown of hers. In truth, who cares? I take a shower, dry my hair, and then brush out the stringy layers I wish would curl of their own volition. Bare-faced and clean, I put on my blue T-shirt and white shorts, grab my room key, and am out the door before she can change her mind.

When I reach the entrance of the hotel, Ray is nowhere to be seen. I hear a car honk its horn outside and follow the noise with my eyes until I find Ray getting out of a white two-door convertible and jogging to the passenger side to open the door for me. He is wearing white shorts that come down to his knees and a light blue button-down shirt that matches the blue in his eyes. I try to hide the thrill rising from my throat like a song about to escape through my lips. A few feet taller than me, he bends down to kiss my cheek, and I conceal the rush of heat rising to my cheeks by turning away from him and stepping into the car that awaits me.

In all the years my mother and I have traveled and all the countries we've been to, we have never rented a car, so this is a treat. I have learned that the same mother who has complete command over me does not navigate driving with the same kind of ferocity or confidence. She is a timid driver, shaky behind the wheel, trailing along the right lane of the highway while cars speed past her driving the minimum speed limit. Ray maneuvers the convertible around the bends and curves along the long stretch of the Honolulu strip as if he has memorized it, and I wonder how many girls he has taken out on a similar excursion.

"You seem to know this area quite well," I point out.

"Yeah, I've been driving every day, taking my mom and sister shopping and sightseeing. It's easier than waiting around for cabs and buses. It's fun driving, not like navigating my way around Brooklyn and the city. This is so restful."

I settle back into my leather seat, satisfied with his answer, taking in the blur of lights and sounds that zip past us, making me dizzy.

"Do you want to drive?"

"No!" I cry out sharply. "I don't have my license yet."

"What?"

"I know," I laugh at the disbelief in his voice. "I got my permit when I turned sixteen, and I tried driving in Queens with my mom, but she was petrified and hasn't let me back behind the wheel since. In all honesty, I don't want to drive. It's scary. And I know the subway system like the back of my hand. There isn't anywhere I want to go that I can't take the train to."

"Makes sense," he says, "but it would also give you freedom. Like right now, you could be driving instead of hanging out with your mom in the hotel room. Trust me, I know."

I toss him an agreeable smile, my gaze finding his hands, long and strong, as they turn the wheel, controlling the white hunk of metal simply with his fingertips.

After what seemed like a long, breezy drive, Ray pulls into the parking lot of a local burger joint.

"You like burgers?" he asks.

"Who doesn't?" I laugh, letting him guide me through the parking lot and the doors leading into a small but bustling restaurant. We both order the same thing, cheeseburgers, well done, with fries and coleslaw on the side. Sipping our Cokes, the conversation between us doesn't dawdle as it tends to among strangers, and I am at ease with him, words coming out of me with the precision and confidence I often lack with people I don't know very well.

When we exit the place, he grabs my hand, and it rests in the palm of his without protest, my skin tingling with anticipation.

"Want to walk on the beach for a bit?"

I nod, mute. My entire body knows what will come next, and I am looking forward to it. I want to kiss him, wondering if I will find salt from the ocean's air on his lips and the remnants of Coke on his tongue.

Taking off our flip flops, we hold hands, swinging them gently as we walk side by side, wordlessly strolling along the water's edge, the warm, wet sand squeezing between our toes. Occasionally, our hips bump into each other of their own free will, insistent on generating the rush of adrenaline that emanates from my pores and gets caught in my throat, filling my mouth with a need I don't know is there until it rushes into my throat and I want to laugh or cry or howl into the dark skies crowding over me.

When we reach a spot on the beach inhabited only by the two of us, Ray looks down at me, places his fingers on my chin, and pulls my mouth up to his. On my tippy toes already, I arch my body towards his, fitting all of me into him, so that I can reach his lips and have my first taste of him. Placing an arm around my waist, he bends to his knees and pulls me down to him, both of us searching for the cool, curvy sand-bed that will bear our weight. Nestled in the sand, into each other's arms, we kiss, our lips and tongues searching for succor as if we have never been kissed before—as if all the answers to life's turbulence and arbitrariness is hiding somewhere in there, in the deep caverns of our mouths, where love resides, waiting to be unearthed and discovered.

Like Danny, Ray doesn't try to invade my body or touch parts of me covered by modesty and clothing. His fingers brush against my throat, arching my head for a deeper kiss, and his hands run along the sides of my ribcage, teasing their way to my breasts, but never actually getting there. I think I will let him, if he tries, but he doesn't, and I don't have to make a choice, to stop the foreplay that rests on kisses and the sensory overload resulting from a single touch of the neck, the outline of my hips, his fingers tangled in my hair, tugging lightly so that my body pushes harder against his, my hips shifting of their own volition against the hardness they find there. Like with Danny, I am surprised at the natural ways my body folds into desire, knowing how to move and where to press against, without permission or guidance from me. My head works overtime to control my body's tendencies, to restrain it from drifting into currents that can overwhelm me, pull me towards a course I am not ready or willing to consider. It is all too much, and I only want this part— the kissing, the vigorous breathing, longing coming up for air, fingers tantalizing skin with an unthreatening variation.

I force myself to slow down, to stop moving against Ray's body, to cool the effects of his lips on my neck, my mouth, my cheeks, his fingers still lingering on my waist, his breath heavy against my hair.

"You're beautiful," he says to me, his blue gaze holding mine while his fingers move strands of hair away from my cheeks. I blush. No one has ever told me I am beautiful. Cute, yes. I am small and fiery, yes. These are the words often used to describe me by girls and boys who know me alike. But never beautiful. It's nice, wonderful even. To be seen as beautiful, to be desired, wanted.

But I want more. No. Not sex. Sex is not enough for me. I want to be loved. And since my own mother has a hard time loving me, I wonder if I can be loved. If she doesn't love me, how can anyone else? How can a boy? Danny said he loved me, but he also loved Helen. He kissed me in my room while he was still dating her. That's not love. And this—this thing with Ray—is not love, either.

I'm not stupid. I'm not one of those girls who fools herself into thinking that sex means anything remotely close to love.

This is sex even if we're not having any yet. This will lead to sex if I let it. But I won't. Not unless it comes with love, and love comes first. Or nothing.

So, I let the word "beautiful" slide off my heated skin like a single drop of water that does nothing more than cool me off. I enjoy his kisses, the attention, his body wrapped around my own, but that is all this is and nothing more. It is fun, exciting, new. Ray is gorgeous and sexy, and his eyes keep inviting me to lose myself, but I am too hardened to believe in the fantasy of finding love in Hawaii. With a stranger. For one night.

Virgin doesn't mean naive or simple. It means resolved, particular, decisive. Love will win out, not sex, not seduction, not a twenty-year-old boy with cool sea-colored eyes and a gentle touch. My body obeys, her limbs yielding in surrender to her mother and master. We wait for love. She concedes.

"I can't believe I had to come all the way to Hawaii to find you, even though you live thirty minutes away from me." His words break into my thoughts. Sitting up, he pulls me closer to him, my ear against his chest, listening to the vibrations of his breathing as they settle into a calm, pacified rhythm. We watch the light from the moon reflect upon the ocean's surface before us, all of us cradled in quiet, in stillness, undisturbed by the vibrant and wild happenings of the past hour on its sandy shores.

I nod. "Funny," I whisper, not sure what it all means and not wanting to break the spell of the moment by digging into labels and definitions. I am content right now, in this isolated space and time, and I don't need anything else or anything more.

The ride back to the hotel is quiet, with Ray's fingers clasped in mine the entire trip, his free hand maneuvering the wheel with expertise as we speed through the darkness of the road away from our fantasy, nearing a reality that is built around our mothers and a home far away from sunsets and walks along the beach.

Back at the hotel, Ray parks the car and guides me to the pool nestled in the back with a trail that leads to the hotel's private beach area. Not wanting to go back to our rooms and end the evening, we sit next to each other on a lounge chair and kiss again. This time, our kisses aren't hurried or explosive; they are slow and tender, exploring, asking, forming promises of a tomorrow that will find the same two people in a whole other setting, not as romantic, but still full of longing.

THE VIRGIN REVISITED

A week after my return to New York, Ray calls me for a date. I am nervous. I expect he wants to revisit or pick up where we left off in Hawaii. It was fun in Hawaii. We were strangers, unattached to each other. There had been no expectations. We didn't know if we would see each other again, so there was no pressure. This time, at home, where we can possibly see each other again and again, I begin to feel the weight of pressure that builds up in my chest and makes me bite my nails until I taste blood.

When he picks me up, it is not in a shiny white convertible, but a Honda Acura that blares its horn, a command to go downstairs and enter its dark depths without knowing what will await me there.

My mother is at a dinner banquet with her Japanese Club, somewhere in Chinatown, where they meet and eat together every couple of months. She isn't Japanese, but her best friend Nana is, and the club has adopted my mother as one of their few white members. I run downstairs, take a deep breath to calm myself before I open the main door leading to the street, lock the door behind me, and then stroll to his car, the engine rumbling in rhythm to the house music that wails from the open windows. I am glad my mother is not around, because she would definitely have something snarky to say about him not ringing the doorbell, not asking to come up to see her, not opening the car door for me, and not having the courtesy to lower the wild sounds of music disturbing our quiet neighborhood. I have the same thoughts, and the romantic halo that had encircled the memory of Ray begins to retreat as soon as he honks his horn at me, calling me out from the serene interior of my home.

Because the music is so loud, we can't talk, but he holds my hand as he speeds along Woodhaven Boulevard to take me to a rib place in Howard Beach. We sit opposite each other at the table, laughing at the messiness of BBQ sauce on dates, his fingers reaching out to clip a bit of sauce from my chin. After a while, I am exhausted from eating ribs. It takes too much energy to eat without seeming sloppy, and I don't want to appear like a slob in front of Ray, who is eating his ribs with expert fingers. I focus my attention on my fries, picking up one at a time, dipping it into ketchup, and then taking small, gingerly bites from each one. At one point, he smiles at me, leans over the table, and plants a quick kiss on my mouth, birthing a deep and knowing smile on my face.

"Come on," he says once he pays the bill. "I have a surprise for you."

Grabbing my hand, he pulls me out of the restaurant, back into his car, and drives in and out of the brightly lit lanes of the boulevard until he makes a left turn into the quiet neighborhood whose homes rest near the water. He parks the car, pulls me out of it, and guides me to a small, remote sandy area that overlooks the beach. Kneeling on the sand, he pulls me down, and our bodies pick up where we had left off in Hawaii. We roll over the hard, grainy bed laid out before us by nature and kiss, first hard and deep, then slowly, our lips and tongues becoming reacquainted with the desire they find there. When we get back into the car and head to my home, where I know my mother will be waiting for me, I am covered in sand, quietly noting all the areas I will need to ensure the sand doesn't remain, like inside my shorts and underwear.

When we near my house, he parks the car a block away instead of dropping me off at my door. Turning the engine off, he leaves the music on and reaches over to me to take me in his arms and kiss me. There is urgency in his movements, a persistence that takes me off guard and then puts me on guard. His fingers aren't patient this time, not at home, where he is comfortable and in control—and I am no longer a stranger in his embrace. He knows me. He knows I like him, and his body moves into mine, pressing against me with a heaviness that leaves me struggling for air, his hands roving over my breasts, my hips, my buttocks, with a hunger I don't want to satiate with my body. I like it. I do. His touch on me leaves me breathless and giddy, drawing new sensations from my stomach and chest, my breasts prickling and arching under his caresses, reaching for his fingers against my own will, but it is too much, too soon. I'm not ready, and I don't want to be ready. Not for this. Not for what will eventually come between us if I let him do what he wants now, our first date away from the romantic and heady interlude we found away from home—and in Hawaii of all places.

I pull away from him slowly, wanting more of the kissing— the slow and the hard and the deep—without the touching and all those intense feelings that spring from a single graze of his fingers on my skin. My mouth takes his with hunger, but each time, his hands skirt around my body, forcing me to place distance between us again.

"Can't we just kiss?" My words come out in bursts.

"Yes. But can't we do more?" He counters.

"Look," I tell him. "I'm a virgin. I'm not ready for more."

He looks at me then and I watch as his smile widens, showing me straight, white teeth I have slid my tongue over with teasing licks. "I can teach you."

I realize just then that my virginity is bait, not a boundary. I want to use it to protect me from roving hands and greedy boys who only want my sex without an investment in the girl, but boys don't see it as armor, necessary, and something to behold with respect. They see it as a challenge, something they must conquer. To be the first to plant a flag and a seed. To say, "I was here first." A hard-earned medal acquired by smooth talk, relentless convincing, and paid-for dinners.

And then what? When they win my virginity, what am I left with? Nothing? They will eventually leave, because every beginning has an ending, off to conquer some other body, and I will have nothing to be proud of, nothing to call my own, nothing to mark me as different and special. They take, and I give and give? Is this what relationships are? Then I don't want them—or the lovely-looking boys whose kisses feel like love until you say no, forcing the real thing to come out and look like nothing more than lust and entitlement.

Ray's attitude makes me feel more respect for myself, makes me more faithful to myself. I'm not afraid that he won't call me again. I enjoy his kisses, but I don't see this going anywhere except to sex, and I'm not going to have sex with anyone just because it is expected. Just because they want it. If I don't want it, it won't happen. I'm not going to give myself away to someone because he kisses well or because his mouth on mine is ravenous and delicious. I decide right there and then that if a guy wants me—that is to say, loves me—then he will have to wait for me until I am good and ready to want him back in that same way.

We wait for love. My body sighs, but she concedes.

"I'll call you." Ray drops me off in front of my apartment. He kisses me again, this time with a gentle touch of my lips, his mouth lingering on mine with his promise, but my heart has already closed access to him, my flesh grown cold and immune to his touch. I shut him out without saying a word, a trick I have learned from my mother, retreating into myself, my thoughts, able to stand before people without being there. I have already left him at the curb, even though my body is going through the motions of exiting his car, shutting the door behind me, and walking to the hard and wooden frame that will lead me back into my own home. Where I am safe and just as unloved.

Ray doesn't call. Small parts of me are disappointed—my lips, my mouth, my fingers—parts of me that miss human contact. The rest of me acknowledges that this is what happens when you say no to sex.

A few months later, I am downstairs doing laundry and hear my neighbor from the second-floor apartment trudge down the stairs.

"Hi, Mr. Isaac," I call out behind me as I kick the mounds of dirty clothes from the hallway into the boiler room where the washing machine and dryer are kept. Both machines belong to my mother, and I come down every weekend to catch up on my laundry. With one load in the dryer and one in the washing machine, I turn around to greet him with a smile.

He stops before me, looking uncomfortable, shuffling his brown leather loafers before extending an envelope towards me.

"My wife and I," he hems and haws, "we try to keep to our business, but we didn't think this was right, so here." He pushes the envelope at me again, urging me to take it. My hand lifts mechanically to grasp it and I catch sight of my name on the front of the envelope. It is addressed to me. "Return to Sender" is scribbled in the center in my mother's elegant and loopy handwriting. Ray's full name and his Brooklyn address are on the sender's corner.

I push my eyes back to the wrinkled, kind eyes of the man who stands before me, a man who keeps his distance and only speaks to me and my mother when he has to—like now—caught unaware of the circumstances in which I find myself. Aside from saying hello or goodbye when our paths meet in the hallway or on the stairs, we are all a bunch of strangers sharing a few spaces within the brick building we call home in Elmhurst, three blocks in from Queens Center Mall, a local movie theater, a series of Chinese and Cuban restaurants, the subway station where the G makes local stops, and a hub of buses that take people to surrounding areas of Queens like Astoria, Flushing, Rego Park, Forest Hills, and Howard Beach without getting on the highway that diverges and leads to Manhattan if you head west and Long Island if you drive East. We live in the same building, share the same spaces of our home, but we are all foreign to each other. This is what my mother wants, and we all abide by the rules of contact she has established for us. Until now, when Mr. Isaac crosses the red line to tell me that my mother has betrayed my rights, my privacy. As if any of these values have ever belonged to me—been given to me for free.

"I don't want to get in the middle of whatever is happening between you and your mother, but I found this outside, by the mailbox. I saw your name on it and that it was opened, and I thought it was only right to give it to you." Mr. Isaac's voice breaks through the fog that overtakes me. "It's not right for your mother to keep this from you. You have a right to read your own mail."

"Okay," I muster when I can find my voice again.

He looks at me as if he wants to say something more. But like me, he can't seem to find the words. He pats my shoulder, and I note the freckles peeking out from beneath the dark hairs on his arm.

"Alright then. You take care," he tells me, plodding back up the stairs where he will lose himself behind the door of the apartment he shares with his wife, becoming an unfamiliar again.

I crawl back into the boiler room, my knees weak beneath the slight weight of my movements, close the door behind me, and find comfort in the three-by-three foot dimensions of the small space, leaning against the vibrating lulls of the washing machine as it rolls the clothing back and forth without missing a beat.

Ray has written me a letter. And my mother has taken it, read it—based on the scotch tape that covers the envelope lid—and placed it outside of our mailbox so the mailman can find and return it without me ever knowing of its existence.

My hands are shaking as I reopen the envelope and begin to read Ray's scratchy writing.

Dear Kathy,

I'm sorry it's taken me so long to get in touch with you. I wanted to call you. So many times. But something always held me back. Being with you was amazing. I love talking to you, and you make me feel things I don't feel when I'm with other girls. My mom and Lillie love you and you know my mom was talking to me about you, saying how dumb I was to let you go. That you could be the one. And I think this is what scares me. I didn't call you because if I did, and we kept going out, we would get serious, and that scares me. I know you're just eighteen, but I'm just twenty, and I'm not sure I'm ready for all of that. But I want to try. I want to be with you, go out with you, have you as my girl-friend, hear you call me your boyfriend. I don't know what the future holds for us, but I know that I miss you and I want to be with you. Please write to me or call me. Let me know if it's okay for me to call you. I know I messed up by not calling you. So much time has passed since I last saw you, but I still think about you. I want to see you again, bring you to my house, visit with my family, get to know your mom. Everything. Give me another chance. Please. Call me.

Love, Ray

Pulling the letter to my chest, I take deep breaths, trying to slow down my heart from racing. Anger burns in my throat and I want to scream, to punch something hard, to fill the hollowness inside me with something, even if that something is pain.

Abandoning my laundry, I yank the boiler room door open and storm up the two flights of stairs leading to the apartment I share with my mother. The letter still clasped between my trembling fingers, I search for my mother, locating her in her office, sitting behind the sewing machine she uses to make her own clothes for work.

"What's this?" I lift the hand still clutching the letter, making sure that I don't push it at her, afraid she will take it from me, and I will never see it again. She has great skill in taking things from me and making them disappear, like friends and tokens of affection given to me by people I have loved and letters professing a love for me she has never professed in words or on paper.

"You weren't supposed to find that." She doesn't look at me as she takes three pins out from between her lips and places them on the fabric she is stitching together.

"Well, I did." I don't tell her about Mr. Isaac. I don't want to put him in the middle, make my mother hate him, or worse, evict him.

"He's not good for you," she begins, this time casting a pointed look at me from above the rims of her glasses resting on the bridge of her nose. "I thought it would be better for you to return his letter."

"That should be my choice," I raise my voice to her, still indignant. "Why can't you trust me to make my own decisions? I know what I'm doing."

"Do you?"

"Yes, I do."

"Well, I don't think you make the best choices for yourself. You don't seem to have very good judgment when it comes to people you surround yourself with." She isn't looking at me anymore.

"I have excellent judgment."

She doesn't look up. She doesn't respond.

"Don't invade my privacy again," I warn her.

"Kathryn," she begins. "This is my home and as long as you live here, I have a right to know everything you're up to."

"Well, my relationships are not your business," I remark and storm out of her office before she can say anything else. As usual, nothing is accomplished. Resolutions don't occur or exist in my interactions with her. It's her home. Her rules. And as long as I live with her, I belong to her.

Angry, I slam the door of my room shut, letting her know

that she is not welcome to enter or disturb me. Now for Ray.

Sitting down at my desk, I take out my pen and draft a letter to him. I tell him that as sweet as his letter is, we both know he hasn't called me because I won't have sex with him. And this is okay. I tell him that at eighteen, I am not ready for sex with anyone. I want to go to school, educate myself, and get a full-time job, and that this is more important to me than sex or having a relationship with him. I tell him I will never forget Hawaii, but that it was a fantasy, and this fantasy is over. Reality has set in, and he should find himself a girl his age who wants what he wants. That girl is not me. I tell him goodbye. I sign my name, place the letter in an envelope, and walk it down the block to the nearest blue mailbox. Opening the chute, I toss it in and then close the lid shut with a resounding finality whose echo pursues me days after I have walked away.

My mother cannot find it here. She can't pull it out, read it, amend it, and not send it. It's gone. And so is my romance with Ray. He never calls again, and no letter ever arrives in my name. At least, none that I am aware of. Who knows how many letters she has intercepted and withheld from me? This is only one instance that I have become aware of, and my neighbor has brought it to my attention. I am too tired to think about stopping her actions. I let her be. I don't look at the mail. This is a fight I will not win, and I don't want to know what she does with mail coming to me in my name. I don't want to fight with her, fight against her. It's too tiresome. She's too tiresome. I can only control myself, my actions, and I can only plan for a future that will remove me from under her rigid thumb.

I give in. I wait. And I plan.

THE EDUCATION OF A VIRGIN

I am in my first year of Queens College in Flushing, majoring in English literature. I spend my days in school, hanging out at the Quad, going from course to course. I work the morning shifts as a page at the local library, returning books to their respective shelves on the stacks, and organizing them by the Dewey decimal system. It's a quiet job, and I find myself lost in thought, reading a few pages of books before putting them in their homes for someone else to find them.

I love the smell of books. I've had this job since I was sixteen, since I first came in and discovered that this was a job and being a page was a position that would suit me perfectly. I don't make a lot of money, but I love being among books, smelling the musty scent of them, wondering who has held them and how they had been moved by the story hiding between the covers, being exposed to words and language and phrases that catch me off guard, make me think about how words can be strung together in unique ways that force me to examine my life, my choices, my selfhood. I love the freedom I have in this job, the quiet, being spoken to only when I am asked to locate a book for a patron or when a librarian asks me to work behind the counter. Because I have been working with them for two years now, they allow me to check books out for our patrons, a job usually conducted by the librarians. They even let me sit in the back, taking books people have dumped into the return chute, setting them up to be delivered to their rightful owners: Flushing Public Library, Jamaica Public Library, Forest Hills Public Library, and so on. The librarians know they can count on me, and I can count on this job, my first job ever, and one that I am hard-pressed to abandon, even when I find a job that pays me better.

It is my first year in college, and I have found my small army of friends in the Honors in Western Civilization classes we share. They are Jewish, and we are nerds together. They adopt me, a Greek Orthodox girl, and invite me to hang out with them at their Jewish Club located in the basement of the Student Union. The school has a Greek Club, but I don't have any Greek friends. My friends are all Jewish, so I hang out with them in school and out. They provide me with a place to rest between my classes; a place where I become a regular body, a familiar face they all say hi to, sit next to and eat lunch with. I spend all my time here. I study here, I live here, I find more friends here who invite me to bars in the city, offer to pick me up in their cars and give me a ride to a party, knowing I don't have a car of my own. They're fun and smart and they listen to my stories about my mother. They know why I hate going home, why I throw myself into school and work. They hug me and tell me they love me, and I learn to say the words back to people I have grown to trust with my feelings and my heart. They give unconditionally, and I learn that giving is offered without asking for anything in return. I haven't known that. My mother does not give without expecting something in return. I have not known giving as a gift without chains and conditions attached to the tags and bows used to decorate it.

On Thursday nights, the student union has parties hosted by individual clubs. No matter which club hosts it, we all head to the main dining hall each week and move to the dance floor like a swarm of yellow jackets gathering, dancing to the raucous music the DJ plays. I dance with Alan, a piano prodigy who can play music on the black and white keys with his feet. I dance with girls and guys in groups and in pairs, and this is where I learn to use my dancing legs, where I learn to love music and the feel of it on the slight curves of my body, feeling my body surrender to the beat without thought or concern. Without alcohol. Without judgment or ridicule when my sea legs are getting used to freestyle moves not attached to the circular dancing of Greek festivals I grew up participating in while in Greek school during my primary years.

It is after one of these student union events that my mother picks me up from campus and drives me home. Matthew, a friend of mine, is supposed to take me home, but when we arrive at his car, he has a flat tire. He calls his dad to bail him out, and I call my mom to pick me up. It's eleven thirty in the evening on a weeknight.

When my mom pulls up in her army green Chevy, she is quiet until I settle into the passenger seat and she pulls off Kissena Boulevard and bears a left onto the congested lanes of the Long Island Expressway leading us west.

"What were you doing that your friend got a flat tire?" She begins the conversation without looking at me, her knuckles white and taut as they grip the wheel.

"What do you mean?" I am perplexed by the question.

"Exactly that." She pulls her eyes off the road to catch a glimpse of mine.

"What? You think we were having sex or something? How do you get a flat tire while having sex?" I ask, shaking my head with fury.

"Well, you had to be doing something." My hands are fisted on my lap.

"We weren't doing anything, Ma. We walked to the car and noticed his front tire was flat. He called his dad to help him out, and I called you for a ride. That's all." The veins on my neck begin to pulse and vibrate, and I think they will burst.

She arches her penciled-in eyebrows and gives me a pointed look that reminds me I am a liar and she can't believe anything I say. Meanwhile, I won't lie. Not to her. I spend much of my time divulging too much information about my friends to her, about my job, my schoolwork, to show her I trust her, I love her. I tell her everything—even though she uses it against me. I ask her to trust me in return, to accept me, but she doesn't know how: how to give in to me, to believe my words, to trust my actions. She thinks I am a whore—at eighteen. I tell her who I am, but she doesn't see me. She only sees what she wants, what she believes me to be. Not me. I want to give up trying to persuade her, but I don't know how. I love her. I need her. I'm afraid to leave her, to exist without her, even if I am nothing while living with her. I know I will not be complete until she sees me and accepts me— maybe even loves me.

After a heavy pause, she begins again.

"I want you to be home by eight o'clock on weeknights from now on. This is unacceptable, having to pick you up at eleven thirty at night from whatever it is you're doing."

"Ma, I am home by eight every night, except Thursday nights. I don't have classes on Friday. And I'm hanging out at school—not clubs or bars. There's no drinking, just dancing."

"I don't know what's going on here, and it's still a school night. You should be at home, studying, not staying out this late. If you're not careful, you're going to turn out just like your mother. A whore."

The words grind into me like a bullet shot out of a revolver. It's not the first time she has said these words to me. In the past, I would retort with, "You're my mother. Are you calling yourself a whore?" To which she would purse her lips and remind me, "We both know I'm not your real mother."

"I'm eighteen, for God's sakes. You have to trust me," I say instead, not wanting to fight the same old fights that have no resolution but are intended only to remind me of the dregs of my origins—origins that have nothing to do with her and will not be reflected on her if I go down the wrong path—like becoming a whore.

"Well, that's the right word. Trust. You have to earn my trust. It's not something you're given for free."

"And I haven't earned it?"

"No, you haven't."

"What must I do to earn your trust then? Obviously, going to school and graduating second in my class, getting all A's, and not dating until I'm eighteen is not working for me."

"By doing what is expected of you without me having to tell you."

This conversation, like all our conversations, will go around in circles, without an end or a beginning. There is no compromise. No discussion. Just submission. One concession after another until I no longer exist. Until my will is crushed, and I sit before her still as an automaton, acting only as she wills me to.

"Well, I don't think I have to do any more to earn your trust. I go out with my friends, on my school campus, once a week, and I don't think there's anything wrong with this. I'm not drinking, not doing drugs—I'm not even dating anyone—so there's no reason not to trust me. I'm not stupid, and I have no intention of doing anything that will ruin my life. If you can't trust me, then there's nothing more I can do. This is all you—your problem—not mine." I cross my arms across my chest and look out the window at the obscured stream of lights that zip past us. We are on the highway, but my mother drives in the right lane—the slow lane—at fifty miles an hour, cars racing past us in a dizzying blur.

"If you continue to go out during the week and come home late, I will not pay for your school tuition," she warns me with a tone that tells me she is serious.

My mother likes ultimatums. At some point, she learned the secret she needed to control me: That I am afraid. Of everything. Of losing her. Of being alone. Of being abandoned. Of not having a home. And this time, of not having my education. I need school. It is the only thing I know that will provide me the freedom I need to get a job and move out of her home—away from her clutches, her ultimatums, that look of disappointment she gives me when she thinks I'm not aware of her watching me over the visible curve of her bifocals. Now she uses my education to threaten me, to control me, to keep me in line. Is there anything that she won't use against me?

"Then don't pay for school," I tell her. I can feel my heart pounding beneath my skin, trying to push past it, through it, in a scream of protest. But I drive my words forward, past the fear stuck in my throat like vomit that doesn't quite come out but stays there, making me gag without reprieve. "I'll pay for it myself."

"Fine," she concedes. "The fall semester is the only one I have paid for. You will have to find the money to pay for the next semester." She is goading me. I have a part-time job at the library that pays nothing, and she knows there's no way I will be able to afford to pay for my school without caving in and asking her for help. She knows I will give in to her, come crawling for forgiveness, be the obedient girl I have served up to her each and every time I find myself invisible in her presence, trapped in the tethered and austere knots of her disapproval like a bug fastened to the sticky webs of a mother-spider awaiting to devour her prey. But I know something else. I know that I will not cave in. I will not submit to her. I will make my own way, and I will earn—maybe not her trust—but definitely my own self-respect.

I bite my nails for two days, and then on Sunday, I begin looking for work. I find a job at Sears in the mall on 63rd Street in Rego Park, fifteen minutes away from the library on foot. Because they both pay minimum wage, I decide I need both jobs to pay for school, but this is all my money will go to after I squeeze enough to pay my mother $100 a month for my bed and the water I use for my daily showers. I believe that by giving her money, I will be afforded the freedom I need to become my own person, to shred the umbilical cord she keeps chained to my feet, to force her to see me as an adult worthy of her trust.

I go through training at Sears, learning how to work a cash register and then patrol the floor in the luggage department. I hate the register and handling money, so I ask my supervisor to let me organize the floor, pulling the luggage from one section to the next, helping customers and keeping the displays neat and tidy. I enjoy this job. Like the library, it is mostly quiet. I work the night shifts, from 5:00 p.m. to 9:30 p.m., closing time, so I spend much of my time picking up items that customers have misplaced and relocating them to their respective areas. Between school and work, I feel productive, confident, busy. I realize that I am adaptable, I can be trained to learn new skills, and I am a quick learner. My supervisors like me, commend me on my work ethic, and recommend me for tasks that require trust—trust I can easily find in strangers and employers but not in the one woman who has known me almost all my life.

It is at Sears one night that I look up from the scarves section I'm organizing to find Nana, my mother's best friend, standing opposite me, watching me. Nana is Japanese, the weight of her obese body having forced her to walk with a cane, and a social worker. Nana has been there since the beginning, disrupting the contentious relationship between me and my mother by taking me away from the city to Saratoga Springs, where her brother and his wife live. I spend many weekends there, eating with them as if I am part of their family. They take me to the local markets, fairs, and library events, and give me the space I need away from my mother when I'm in high school, when breathing beneath the weighty wings of her domineering parenting is stifling and almost impossible for a girl who has no skills in interpreting the actions of adults around her.

Her brother, Toyo, teaches me to drive the tractor he uses to cut the lawn on his expansive land with an old Victorian home falling apart at the seams but still standing like an old man whose spine is folding in on him, stooped and aloof. The top floor is off-limits to everyone in the house; no one goes up there, fearing that the ceiling will cave in from water damage and the floors will crumble. The dark oak floorboards creak and whine under the pressure of their spaniel Coco's claws clicking against wooden floors when she sneaks past the barricaded stairway. No one dares to go up the stairs to retrieve her. They use dog biscuits to coax her back to the safety of the second floor, adding old, tattered books to the wall they have made up of chairs and boxes to ward off the inviting path to danger she always seems to find, her nose sniffing past the walled items for another entryway.

Because Nana is a social worker who has her own office in Brooklyn, she makes time to talk to me throughout the years. I am ten when I first begin to think she is my friend, that she cares for me, so I tell her how I feel. We are sitting in McDonald's where she has taken me for a one-on-one talk without my mother present. This is how early on in my adoption our problems begin. I tell her that my mother called me a liar when I tried telling her about my birth mother: her violent rages as she beat my father, the pimp that took his place. But my mother did not want to hear it. She told me I was full of lies and that she would not listen to me. I try to say more, but Nana cuts me off.

"That's ridiculous," she scoffs. "Your mother would never say that. Never!"

And I learn that Nana is not someone I can talk to. She is my mother's friend, even though she sits in front of me and assures me she's here for me, to help me. So, I talk to her only when I must, but I hide the parts of me she doesn't want to know exist—the parts that show her how my mother mothers me—what she doesn't see or hear after she leaves. I go to Saratoga with her because I have to—I have no choice. I help her move boxes from one apartment to another, I carry books and other items from her car into her new office, I smile at her across the table situated between us at a restaurant we all meet for dinner, and I sit beside her at the Japanese Club's annual banquets because I am required to, by her, by my mother. But I don't speak to her from my heart. She won't believe me. And like my mother, she doesn't want to know what hides in there.

So when I raise my eyes from the display table of scarves I'm folding at Sears one Saturday night during my shift to find her standing before me, a surprised smile overtakes my mouth. "What are you doing here?"

"I know what you're doing." Her tone is low and cold as it strokes my skin.

"What?" Shock finds root in my brows, freezes my smile. I shake my head, thinking I have misunderstood her. I bend my shoulders forward to listen with more care.

"I know what you're doing. To your mother. You're not fooling me. You're not fooling anyone."

I have taught my body to go cold, slack, and I apply this trick right now. It's a trick I have learned from my dealings with my mother when she comes at me out of nowhere with some kind of accusation that attempts to define me but doesn't fit me. It's like I am invisible. I force my thoughts to disappear. They can throw words at me, but I am not there. I cannot take them into me. They go through me and disappear into the ether. It appears that Nana has also acquired lessons from my mother: the art of ambushing with words—cryptic words that accuse and lack specificity.

I run my absent eyes over Nana, my features blank and void of expression, toss the scarves in my hand back into the display unit, and walk away from her, my back strong and straight. I go to another display, but she follows me, saying nothing. Each time I move, she moves. I pretend she's not there. I will my hands to stop shaking, my legs to hold me upright, for all I want to do right now is sink to my knees and cry.

Eventually, she leaves, and I turn slowly to watch her retreating back. She is not my friend, and this time, I know it for good.

I watch her large body glide upwards on the escalator, and it's not until all of her disappears from my sight, that l can let myself go. My limbs loosen from my bones, and I waver, my hands reaching out to grip the edges of the table before me. I open my mouth and a garbled sound erupts. A sob. I can't stop. Janet, a young girl my age working in the area, finds me this way —heaving, gasping for air, tears gushing from my eyes and onto my face with uncontrollable spasms overtaking me.

"I can't stop," I half-cry, half-laugh when she places her arm around me and peers into my face. She phones the night manager, Camille, a middle-aged, beautiful African American woman who comes to work each shift with perfect make-up, dress suits, and high heels. She takes one look at me, puts her arms around my shoulders, and guides me to her office. I am thankful that it is almost closing hour and there are few customers there to witness the mess that is me.

Placing me on the chair by her desk, she sits opposite me and reaches over to me.

I apologize over the sobs. I can't stop them. They just keep coming, as if they have been vibrating beneath the surface for months, waiting for the opportunity to exhaust themselves. It makes sense. I have been working nonstop, trying to save up for next semester. I work in the mornings, go to my classes, and then take the Q60 bus to the mall to work my night shift. The library won't let me work over twenty hours a week, but Sears will, so I work on the weekends as well.

"Can you tell me what happened?" Camille asks softly.

"It's ridiculous," I hiccup, still gulping for air. "My mother's friend came by, said some stupid things to me, and then I just lost it." I try to take deep breaths to calm myself, but the crying resumes and my body is convulsing.

"Was it a man? Her boyfriend?" I shake my head, seeing where she is going. No. It isn't that bad. It's only Nana.

"It's her friend. A woman. I just didn't expect her." This comes out in spurts, but it makes me realize how ridiculous the situation is. Why am I making such a fool of myself? Why can't I just stop crying? "Can I go home now?" I ask Camille, hoping she will just let me go so that I can hide again.

"Kathy, I can't let you leave like this. Can someone come and pick you up? A friend?"

"My friend, Sheila. I'll be okay. I'll just go to her house. Please," the last word comes out softly, a plea. I am embarrassed, and I just want to get out of there. Now.

"Okay, but only if you promise to call me tomorrow, or better yet, come and see me. I have to know you made it home safe." Camille places her fingers on my shoulder and squeezes, and I wonder why my own mother can't express this kind of sympathy to me. I meet a lot of great mothers out in the world, outside of the spaces of me and my life, and I wonder why it is Ann who gets to mother me. Why does she get to mis-mother me?

I am short, but my feet are fast as they take me out of the building and into the street. I move fast across Queens Boulevard, up 63rd Drive, past my library, closed now, to where 63rd intersects with Woodhaven Boulevard. I cry the entire way, my sobs still coming out of me in small, guttural eruptions, as if a bomb goes off inside me every few seconds. I stop at Woodhaven, place a quarter into the phone booth, and call Sheila. When she confirms that she will meet me halfway, I hang up the phone and wait for the light to change. Woodhaven Boulevard is just as wide as Queens Boulevard, with six lanes full of cars zipping at high speed, a blur of white lights and the feeling that one wrong move and you will be flattened by at least three of them before they realize they struck something—someone. It's eight thirty-five in the evening and a middle-aged woman approaches me while I punch the button to make the light change faster. She asks if I need any help, if she should call someone for me. This makes me cry even harder, but I manage to shake my head and say thank you. When the light turns green, I sprint across the lanes, dumbly, blindly, so no one else will take notice of me and ask me if I need anything.

When Sheila and I meet up, it is by a small park made up of trees and benches along the Boulevard. We sit on a bench, and I tell her what happened. She hugs me, and for the first time this evening, my breaths are shallow and my eyes are dry. Nothing else remains bottled up, ready to explode out of me, like opening a bottle of Coke after you shake it too much. I am feeling calm, breathing without the interruptions of hiccupping spasms.

"I called John," Sheila tells me, and I feel like a burden. Everyone who is friends with me gets in the middle of my interactions with my mother. She is the puzzle I can't solve, the problem that persists, and I don't have the experience or objectivity to resolve. So I talk about her and me, and I am sure that I get on my friends' nerves. Sheila thinks John can help me, but I don't want John. He's not the one I called. Our relationship is waning—I am sure he is seeing someone else, but I don't say this to Sheila. I only say, "Thanks."

We walk the fifteen minutes it takes to get to her apartment building, and her mother is there, waiting for us. I don't think her mom likes me. She is tough, severe, and I'm not Indian. When Sheila takes me up to the two-bedroom apartment she shares with her mom and two sisters, her mother looks me over but never says a word to me. She seems to be the Indian version of my mother, except that she did marry a man and is now widowed, raising three daughters on her own, in a run-down and crowded apartment building that overlooks one of the most congested sections of Queens. I don't like going to Sheila's home or being near her mom, but I love Sheila, having met her during my training at Sears, and I spend most of my free time outside her building, walking up and down the street, talking about boys, dating, school, and everything else we can possibly talk about. Sheila is shorter than me, maybe four eleven, with a round brown face, wide brown eyes with thick lashes, and a pair of full lips usually filled in with deep red lipstick. She is fated to marry an Indian boy—whoever her mother insists she end up with—but Sheila likes white boys with chiseled features and wavy dark hair. She sometimes goes on forbidden dates and I cover for her, but her mother has never called me to check up on her. Sheila is my best friend during this time, and like with most of my friends, I curl into the succor of her friendship, escaping the discomfort and loneliness I only encounter in the spaces of my own home and my family of one.

My tears having subsided, I breathe deeply and look out toward the car-lit lanes of the street outlined before us. A long, brown Dodge stops in front of us, and I find my eyes gripped in the intense gaze belonging to John. My chest sinks in a little bit. I know what awaits me, and I am too exhausted to deal with it tonight, but I get up from the bench, hug Sheila, open the door of his car and sink into the worn-out leather passenger seat with mechanical movements. Sheila gives me two thumbs up and a toothy grin that reminds me she is the mastermind who will fix us as if we're broken things with nicks and dents that need repairing. I look at the road ahead of us, an endless road with no end in sight.

A VIRGIN'S FIRST JOHN

When John and I meet, he already has a girlfriend. He is Cuban and Jewish, and he has the features of both cultures playing beneath the dark skin that covers his long limbs, the deep but small brown eyes that make me lose my footing, the wide nose that fans across the backdrop of his face, and the mouth I have grown accustomed to staring at when he smiles at me, his teeth perfectly aligned and white.

A college student majoring in computers, he also works as a security guard in our student union. He's not good looking to most, but I find him beautiful, my senses drawn to him as if he has a magnet in the pocket of his jeans pulling my eyes and hands mechanically to him. He's tall and wide, and everything about him is slow, like a sloth. A sensual sloth. His walk, the way his arms move to and fro when he secures the exits of the building by pacing from one end to the other, his feet dragging along the linoleum floor, his eyes as they take everything in quietly, his smile when it finally arrives, and even his speech—everything about him takes its time to express itself. He's not a big talker, but when he does say something, it is hushed, deep, his voice low and sexy so I have to lean into him to hear what he has to say, inhaling the smell of him when it reaches my nostrils—just as slow and just as deep.

I meet him at the student union one day in between my classes when I enter its corridors in need of coffee and a lounge chair to sink my body into. I find my crew, Chevy and Joe, both college students who work together as mechanics for a major airline in New York. On his break, John sits near us and is eventually pulled into our conversation, since my friend Chevy, another Latino boy with dimples, is more social and chattier than I am. For months, we gravitate to this area of the union building, John's friends and girlfriend mixing with our friends until there is no line separating our two groups and no memory to define how the two groups meshed into one.

I see John everywhere, all the time, and when he talks to me, it seems that his voice and eyes have fingers that touch me. And I know this is wrong because he has a girlfriend, a nice girl named Elena, with black curly hair and brown skin to match his own. They've been together for two years, and they are both older than me by a few years. I don't flirt with John. I'm not good at that yet, and I respect his relationship. I only talk to him when he corners me with his voice, his words fastening me to place and conversation that I find difficult to escape. But I find him looking at me when I least expect it. When I am in the middle of reading my psychology textbook, when Chevy is explaining some algebraic equations I don't get, when I am covering the top layer of my plain yogurt with sugar and then scoop it up with a plastic spoon to eat it.

I find him watching me when I shoot pool, the stick set between my fingers as I blow the solids into corner pockets one by one, smiling when I get to the eight ball, call the pocket, and sink it in without effort. I grin at Chevy, who cheers for me, his dimples deep and wide around his mouth, and then challenges me to another game, which I decline. I have my Great Books course to run to, all the way across the Quad, and I'm already late. Grabbing my backpack, I bolt into the direction of the doors and slam into a hard wall, a chest that stops me, hands that reach out to steady me. I laugh at my clumsiness and feel these spasms trickling up and down my spine and look up to find John's smiling lips warning me to be more careful. I let out a sigh, and I know he knows I like him. How could he not? I freeze in time when he's around. When our eyes lock, it's worse, like we have a private, silent language that we use to communicate and I tell him that I love him and he says, me, too.

I am aware of him, all of him, no matter where I am. When I dance on Thursday nights with Alan, he is there, working, making sure there are no fights and no one under twenty-one is drinking. I am still eighteen and I don't drink yet, but I dance. I am free and wild and fun, and there is no evidence when he looks at me dancing with my friends, getting drunk only on the rhythm and flow of the music that overtakes my limbs, that I am a virgin, a lonely, sad little virgin who loathes going home each and every day's end, who has learned the trick of moving through school and work and dancing and partying and talking to friends without letting anyone in, without letting all of it—all the shit and darkness living inside me—come out and be seen. He doesn't see the crippling emotions, the rage, the loneliness that is me. He only sees the lighthearted girl who laughs aloud at jokes and eats sugar in spoonfuls and shoots pool to win and covers herself in jeans and T-shirts that hug her small curves and he wonders what she looks like underneath the fabric and how she will taste when he kisses her and how her body will move beneath his touch. He imagines a girl that does not exist, and our relationship is doomed from the start, from the moment he breaks up with Elena at the end of the semester, in May, abandons her in the booth that they share, and slides into the one beside me, placing his arm around my shoulders as she watches from the distance of the five feet separating us.

John and I spend the summer together, outside of school, and for the three months that our love lasts, it is blissful and sweet and full of passion and kissing and heavy pressing that never goes beneath the layers of our clothes. He's the first to slide his fingers beneath my shirt, unhook my bra, and touch the peaks of my small breasts, and it takes my breath away each time, my breasts pushing forward into the palm of his hand of their own volition. They want his fingers all over them, and I let them have him. Because he's kind and gentle, I love him, and he is my first boyfriend.

This summer is the best one I've had since Hawaii but it lasts longer. John gives me a circle of new friends, the freedom that comes with having a boyfriend with a car who picks me up every day after his shift ends, takes me to the park, to eat, to play, to his niece's birthday party where I meet his Jewish father and his Cuban mother, who says her hellos with clipped politeness but looks at me as if I come from the wrong side of the tracks. I suppose she feels this way because I am the reason he and Elena break up, but John doesn't say anything about it, except, "She really liked Elena. But she'll like you, too, when she gets to know you. You'll see." He reassures me with a long kiss that makes me hungry for his hands on every inch of my body. His hands are long and bony and brown, and I love looking at them, holding them in mine, kissing the rounded tips when they tug at my hair and travel along the curves of my face, the outstretched length of my throat, my clavicle, the pulsing mounds of my breasts.

When he picks me up, I bring him into my house to meet my mother, trying to force a bridge between the woman I love and the boy I want to get serious with. She is polite and asks him his goals, and she nods her head knowingly when he explains to her he wants to work with computers. Her arched brows tell me she doesn't think much of him, that he is full of talk and not a good prospect for me. But I'm eighteen and not looking to get married. I don't care about his goals after college. I still don't know what I want to do with my degree in English. There's not much I can do with it except teach, and I'm not sure I want to do that yet. Right now, I only want to date John, kiss John, read literature, and eat knowledge in fistfuls without napkins, utensils, or any kind of proper etiquette, licking my fingers at the taste of what I have learned. Having just completed my first year of college, I am only interested in devouring life and new experiences, not thinking about the future or my mother's criticism.

John and I run down the stairs and out of the house, where I find James and Milton in the back seat of John's car. They are his best friends, both nerdy African American boys also interested in the burgeoning field of technology. James has curly hair, is lanky, and has the mannerisms of a twelve-year-old boy. He's young and innocent, and he makes us laugh with inane jokes. Milton is the serious type, bulkier than James, but the two are a pair with Milton pushing his glasses over the bridge of his nose to raise his eyebrows at James's immature antics. They are attached to John and go everywhere with us, and I'm okay with this. They become my friends also, and they act as buffers when I'm not in the mood to be alone with John, when the intensity of his desire is too much, a threat to my self-imposed virginity.

As it happens, I think love will win out, but even with love, I am not willing to give up this thing that makes me feel proud of myself, unique, unused—strong in the face of other people's wants—wants that take pieces of me away from myself. I own my body, and I want to continue owning it. If I give in to John, to the next guy that comes along, I will no longer own this thing that makes me who I feel I am inside—innocent, good, loved. I do love John, but one month, two, even three months of kissing and dating and groping doesn't incentivize me to give up the rest of me to a guy I don't know will be there afterward. So James and Milton joining us makes our evenings stress-free for me because John has been asking for more—not with words—but with the inching along of his fingertips trailing down the line from my belly button to the waistline of my shorts, my jeans, my skirt, which I stop with my own hands pushing his away, kissing him deeply to persuade him to concentrate on other parts of me like my lips, the slope of my outer hips, my breasts. He complies, gives in with a slow sigh released into my mouth so I can taste the disappointment that resides there, the hope I have shriveled in him—until the next time we kiss, the next time we fool around in the back seat of his car, in a deserted parking lot, or two blocks away from my own house, parked in front of a string of homes with the lights out. There's always a next time. Going out with him begins to exhaust me because he keeps trying and I keep resisting.

"He looks like a Cro-Magnon," my mother tells me after he returns me home and peels away from my block, the tires squealing in the distance. She hunches her back, darts her head out from her body, and dangles her arms out and low to show me what he looks like.

"That's mean," I point out to her, over the snorting sounds of her laughter. "Anyway, I'm not with him for his looks. He's nice and smart. And I like him a lot," I add when she looks at me with doubt, her brows arching over her small brown eyes, her lips pressed into a straight, taut line across her face.

"Where do they all take you, he and the two Black boys in the back of the car?" She asks this while peering at me as if my features will reveal to her the truth she anticipates: they're taking turns ravaging me in public spaces, in hotel rooms, in someone's apartment. She examines my face and body for traces of debauchery. She hasn't begun relegating me to the living room couch yet—that comes later—but this is where it begins, her eyes scouring my person for evidence of sex beneath her lashes as I brush my teeth in the hallway bathroom.

I think of John and James and Milton, and I see young boys, innocent ones. There is no drinking, no drugging, no clubbing among us. Being with them is like being free, a kid, having friends to hang out with at parks in Flushing and Woodside, at the movies, sharing a tub of popcorn, watching TV at Milton's house while his mom serves us chips and soda. That my mother looks at them and sees the opposite—indecency, drugs, alcohol, sex even—is unfair and makes me want to hit her hard across her face—to shake reality into her already brittle bones. How can she not see in them what I see, what I know and trust? Why can she not see me, trust that the kind of girl I am would not associate with boys and girls like that? I love innocence, and when I see it in others, I am pulled to it. "You are who you hang out with," she often tells me. I believe in this adage, and I hang out with good people because I am a good person. Ruining my life is not on my list of things to do. Self-destruction is far from my objectives. But the good in me does not exist for my mother. I am who I hang out with, but what she sees is a loose girl getting in the car with three dark-skinned college boys who take her out into the dark and bring her home after midnight, where she crawls into her bed, fatigued and silent.

John is no longer innocent because I am his girlfriend, and I am learning that being someone's girlfriend means being intimate, having sex. It's implied that we will have sex because we're seeing each other. It's implied that I want to have sex with him because I enjoy his kisses and welcome his hands on my bare skin. I am realizing that when he broke up with Elena, with whom he was having regular sex, he assumed he would be giving her sex up for my own. That one will replace the other. This is also implied. But I don't work that way, and he's learning the hard way that my sex, my virginity, is not something I treat as a burden that needs to be shed like the skin a snake outgrows, wriggling out of it in slow, methodical degrees. It is a shield, a strength, a badge of honor, and only love—real love that doesn't come with unrelenting pressure and persistence—will induce me to give it up. To give in. To want more.

I know who I am. I know what I want, and by the end of the summer, persistent hands and begging kisses have gotten on my nerves. Rebuffing him becomes a full-time job and one I am ready to quit.

"Come to my house next weekend," he coaxes, kissing the nape of my neck. "My parents will be out of town."

"Why?" I roll my eyes. "I know what that means, and I keep telling you I'm not ready."

"No, I just want you to see where I live. That's all. Promise."
He kisses me, his tongue probing my mouth until I consent. To
this. To visit his neighborhood, to walk through his house, to sit
on his bed, look over the items in his room. That's all. I'm hard-
core. Saying no is not a hardship for me. The words come out of
me like the incessant flow of blood that visits me each month.
It's natural. It infuses me with anger, with power, with a deci-
siveness I am learning to perceive as belonging to me.

I take the train to Forest Hills, where he lives with his parents. It's Saturday, and they are away for the weekend. Climbing
out of the steaming subway station, I find him waiting for me on
the corner with Coke from McDonald's. I'm a Coke junkie. It's
all I drink, and I favor it over water. I take the drink for what it is
—a testament that he knows me, my quirks, my likes, and dis-
likes. I take a sip from it, hoping he also knows that we won't be
having sex or going further than the slow trailing of fingers
around the nipples of my breasts.

He shows me his house, his room, and when he pulls me to
him, we slowly fall on the navy-blue duvet cover of his bed. I feel
the warmth of him on top of me and respond to his kisses and
touches. I love him. I want him. But only up to a point. Always
up to a point and always the same point. I pry his hands away
from the waistline of my shorts when he tries to lower them
from my waist down to my hips. He takes my hand and places it
on his crotch, still concealed by the shorts he's wearing. In the
three months we've been dating, I have not touched him there. I
have pressed my hips against him while kissing, I have enjoyed
the feel of his genitals pushing into me over our clothing, pin-
ning my back against the cool, hard surface of the wall that
holds me up, but I don't touch him. Until now. Until the mo-

ment he takes my fingers and cups the palm of my hand to the small, hard mound of flesh throbbing against the fabric of his pants, transmitting heat and fear into me. He growls in my ear and brings his hips up to remove his pants.

I grow cold. I pull my hand away from him as if he has burned it.

"I can't," I hiss like a startled cat, raising myself to a seated position on his bed and looking down at him.

"You mean you won't." He clarifies. "I know you want to. What's holding you back? Don't you love me?"

"I do. I do love you. I just don't want to have sex. Not just with you. With anyone. I am not ready yet." I push the bangs away from my forehead and rise from the bed, placing inches of open space between us. I am tired of this conversation. Tired of explaining myself.

"When do you think you'll be ready?"

I shrug my shoulders at him.

"We've been seeing each other for three months. You just turned nineteen. When will you be ready?"

"I have no clue. This is the first time it's come up with anyone. I don't know. I just know I am not there. When I am, I will let you know."

"Well, I may not be around then." He makes sure his eyes meet mine with unwavering insistence.

I turn my gaze over him, finding no trace of the beauty, the easy cadence of attraction that appealed to me three months earlier when he belonged to someone else, when he was safe to love from a distance. If this is what they all turn out to be like in the end, I see no point in dating, in being somebody's girl-friend, in giving so much of myself to them. For what? This anger rising in me like acrid-tasting bile I want to purge from my system?

"Then don't be," is my comeback and I am surprised at the confident coldness I find in my own voice, even though my insides are trembling and on fire. "I'll see you later then." I move to the door.

"I'll walk you to the subway. Wait a second. I can drive you home." He moves as if to rise from the bed.

"No thanks. I know my way back." I leave his house, his neighborhood, and I don't look back to see if he follows me. If he watches me. I want to run, but I force my steps to walk a straight line away from everything that is him.

He calls me a few times. He apologizes for rushing me, he says. School begins, and we sit with each other in our old booth in the cafeteria, laughing and joking with our friends, but there is something between us I can't see or put my finger on. He kisses me, walks me to my classes, but it's not the same. We don't see each other outside of school anymore, and my mother asks what has happened between us.

"He's working," I toss over my shoulder with fake nonchalance. I can't tell my mother the truth. He wants sex and I don't. It's too dangerous to tell her more. She won't believe me anyway. In her eyes, she's the only virgin—the only valuable person in our home.

VIRGIN NIGHTS NEVER END

The night John picks me up from Sheila's house, he drives me to a park in Maspeth, one that we frequented over the summer break, making out on the swings, straddling each other while the swing creaked and swayed beneath the weight of our fervent kissing and touching.

I am quiet, still thinking about Nana, confused about her visit and her words.

"You're like a faucet," John whispers in my ear. We are sitting on a bench side by side. "You run hot and cold, out of nowhere," he explains the comparison when I toss him a puzzled look.

"I'm just thinking," I tell him. I reach over and attempt to kiss him, hoping to disappear into it.

"I think you only want me because it pisses off your mother." He cuts into me, frustration causing his arms to wave wildly in the air before us.

"What? Where's this coming from?"

"You don't want me, Kathy. You kiss me, but you don't want me. Not the way I want you."

"How many times do you need to hear me say it? I love you. I just don't want more than this right now."

"If you really loved me"—his mouth slings the bullshit line I have grown accustomed to hearing from him—"then you would not think twice about sleeping with me."

"And if you loved me," I retort with boredom in my voice, "then you would wait." We're not looking at each other. We're facing the darkness ahead of us, breathing our words into the night air, hoping that someone who cares will catch them, respond to them.

"I still think the only reason you want to be with me is because your mother hates me."

"Well then, you don't know me. I would never hurt myself to hurt my mother. And if that was really the reason, if I wanted to hurt her, I would have sex with you." I say the last few words pointedly, as if I am dragging a dagger across the surface of his skin, slicing into it with malice. I want to hurt him the way he is hurting me. Why can't love be enough? Why can't kissing be enough? Why is sex so important? I want to ask—scream at him —but I don't because there is a part of me that no longer cares.

"I want to go home," I tell him, jumping to my feet. We walk to his car without a word, the next ten minutes of the ride thick with silent phrases we don't share with each other. I get out of his car, heave a long sigh, and enter the framed door of the apartment building I share with a whole bunch of strangers as the peal of his wheels alert me to his withdrawal. I don't look behind me. I only look forward, walking ahead, my steps slow and heavy, wading through layers of muddied pasts and misunderstandings toward the home I dread, the mother I wish would see the girl I am so desperately holding on to for just one drop of appreciation.

Taking each step up to the third floor where I know I will have to face my mother, I stop suddenly, shaking my head to ensure I am really seeing the figure sitting at the top and last step, a big, burly body stationed there, erect and fierce, barring my movements forward.

"What are you doing here?" I scoff at Nana. She sits there, looking at me, an immovable force.

"I want to talk to you," she says.

"What is this, an intervention? Don't you think you've said enough?" I am still reeling from her surprise visit at my job, but I am too tired, too hurt for niceties. "Will you please move so I can go inside? I want to go to sleep."

"I'm not moving, and you're not going inside until you talk to me," she says, widening her eyes at me and smiling without sincerity.

I want to laugh at her but manage to hold it inside. If she thinks any part of me will allow myself to talk to her again, she is delusional. "Have it your way." I smile back. "I can sleep anywhere." With that, I move a few steps back down the way I had come up, sit on one step, and place my head on my arms that I've planted a few steps above me. I fall asleep, the night's events between her and John having exhausted me beyond comprehension. I am awakened by a slight movement above me and the click of the door as it unlocks from the inside. My mother opens the door. They look at each other, and Nana shakes her head. Then she waddles into my home as if she belongs there.

I rise from my mock bed on the stairs, yawn, and look up at my mother, my eyes glossing over hers as they take me in wordlessly. "Can I come in, or do you want to prevent me from going to bed as well?"

She doesn't respond. She only moves back into the threshold

of the home she owns and disappears behind the door. She leaves it open. I can go in. Finally.

As I enter, I find that Nana is sitting on the low-legged, blue-flowered couch in our living room. I don't look at her or my mother, and my feet quickly follow the hallway path that leads me to my room. I slam my door shut and throw my body onto the small frame of my single-sized bed, the old mattress shrinking from the force of my movements.

It's midnight, and my eyes are stinging from fatigue and the immeasurable weight of an evening that doesn't seem to want to end. My door opens, and I watch, stupefied, as my mother walks into my room and stands by the doorway, studying me with keen eyes that believe they will find something, some kind of evidence, if they just keep looking at me, searching my pores with laser-sharp precision. What is she looking for?

"What do you want now?"

"Lower your voice, Kathryn. We don't want to wake the entire neighborhood."

"I don't give a shit about the entire neighborhood," I yell at her, loud enough to make my point. "What is your problem? Did you have Nana come to my work?"

"No, it was her idea."

"And what was the purpose of that? To get me fired?"

"Did you get fired?" She arches her eyebrows in a way that lets me know I am exaggerating.

"No, but it surprised me, her coming to my job while I was working." I don't tell her that Nana's visit made me cry like a baby. I don't tell her that it shook me to the core and that I couldn't stop. I don't want either of them to know how deeply they got to me. "What the hell is this? Why is Nana here? Why did you send her to my job?" I want to cry again, I'm so frustrated, but I gulp all the feelings resurfacing back down like regurgitated bile.

"Kathryn," she begins, and my limbs recoil at the way her patronizing tone slithers and wraps around the syllables of my full name. No one I care about calls me Kathryn. Only Kathy or Kath. She is the only one that calls me Kathryn, and I don't correct her, because I don't want to forget her disapproval of me or slip and trust her when she turns on the sweetness and catches me off guard. Like now, when she approaches me slowly and takes a seat on the corner of my bed, looking at me as if she cares, as if she really sees me, as if she really loves the girl she sees sitting before her, her chest full of longing, starved and denied. "You're never home. You're always out doing God knows what. I am concerned for you, and Nana is only trying to help by coming over here."

"Help!" The word comes out of me in a squeal, and I hope Nana can hear me, still sitting in our living room. She's a school social worker, helping children, and I hope she's better at her job than she is *helping* me and my mother. "She came to my job, stared me down for the longest time, and told me she knows what I'm doing to you. What the hell is that supposed to mean? What am I doing to you? I'm never here. How can I do anything to you?" I swallow back new sobs collecting at my chest and throat. I don't want to cry. Not in front of her. She doesn't know how to handle my emotions. There is never a touch or a hug to soothe the aches away. There is only the distant watching, the gaping, uncomfortable distance she places between us that she doesn't fill with kind words or a smile or a sympathetic caress.

"Nana and I have been talking, and we're worried that you are doing drugs," she finally brings to light.

I freeze. Then offer a laugh. A bitter, distant laugh intended to mock her, saliva collecting inside my mouth that I want to spit into her unyielding eyes. But I hold it in. Swallow it. Like I swallow every insult she hurls at me as if she has never met me.

"I've never done a drug in my life," I sling at her instead, wishing my words were rocks with power to bruise and draw blood.

"Are you sure?" She looks at me in that way she does when she wants to remind me I am a liar. That she does not believe a word I say because my history is set in stony untruths.

"I should know."

"What am I supposed to believe, Kathryn?" She bends her head closer to mine, pushing me further into the pillows behind me. "You leave early in the morning and you don't come home until eleven o'clock at night. You don't eat. You appear gaunt and lethargic when I do see you. Look at your eyes right now. You have dark shadows underneath and you're starting to look old. Older than your age. You look wasted."

"That's because I am exhausted. I work two jobs to pay for school. I go to work in the morning, then school, then to my second job—which you know I have since you sent Nana there to harass me. When would I have time to do drugs? Or money? All my money goes to school and the rest goes to you for rent."

"Well, I would pay for your school, but there would have to be rules about coming home at a decent time," she begins.

"I don't want your money. I like paying my own tuition. I'm tired and stressed, but I have never been prouder of myself." My voice is resolute, and I feel a warm flush surge through me. I am proud of myself, and working for school has taught me that I can do it on my own. That I don't need her money or her home or her to feel secure and independent.

"I don't believe you." Her tone is matter of fact.

"You don't believe that I like paying for school?"

"I don't believe that you're not doing drugs," she corrects.

"What else is new? You never believe me." I push the bangs out of my eyes with trembling fingers and glide my gaze away from her and to the window. It is late, midnight, and all I want to do right now is to fall asleep. My shift at the library begins at 9:00 a.m. but it takes me an hour to get there since I like to walk and not spend my money on the train or bus.

"What am I supposed to believe when you don't talk to me, you come here to sleep and shower, and that's it? And you're always with those hooligans, the Cro-Magnon. You're out at all hours of the night with him and his friends. What am I supposed to think you're doing?"

"Oh, I don't know. Maybe you're supposed to know me, trust me. Trust that I am working like a crazy person just to put myself through school and that the free time I have, I'm either studying or hanging out with my friends." My voice rises a few decibels in my feeble attempt to get her to hear me.

"Kathryn," she warns me, gritting her teeth. "Please keep your voice down. Do you want the entire neighborhood to hear us?" With that, she moves to the window, makes sure it is sealed shut, and draws the blue curtains she sewed on her Singer machine from both sides so that they meet in the middle, enclosing us in darkness, the only light coming from the small lamp I keep beside my bed. "You have to earn my trust," she continues once she's confident that no one else is listening.

I foresee the tangled vine this argument will now pursue. We will talk in circles, echoing phrases we have uttered during many arguments we have had in the past. There will be no resolution.

No new words or concessions will take the place of the old, and everything will remain the same.

"I will never earn your trust. Never. You don't see me. Strangers know me better than you do, and in all honesty, I don't think I care anymore." I sigh aloud and toss my entire body against the mattress, facing the ceiling. My jaw locks, barring any more words from coming out in my defense. They are all for nothing. It's a wasted effort.

She purses her lips in a disapproving line I have come to know very well. "So that's it? You have nothing to say for yourself?"

"You don't believe anything I say, so there is nothing I can say to make you believe me. Are we finished here? I would like to go to sleep. I have work tomorrow." I turn my face to the window, turn off my lamp, and hope my back is a strong enough wall to keep her out.

Eventually, she exits my room like a hushed whisper. I don't even know she is gone until I turn around and don't find her shadow looming over me, staring, analyzing me like a foreign object under a microscope.

HOW TO BREAK A VIRGIN'S HEART

Two weeks later, on a Monday, I am sitting in the booth I share with John and our friends at school.

"It's over," John tells me, not quite looking at me. He places both hands on the wooden backs of the bench and hops over it to the other side of the booth. A quick exit.

Stunned, I look at Chevy, who is pretending to read his English textbook beside me. He casts me a pitiful glance.

"You knew it was coming," he says, reminding me that this is not unexpected. I do. I tell my racing heart to calm down, remind it in turn that this is what we both knew was going to happen. John and I have been playing a game. I've been waiting for him to say the words, and he's been waiting for me. Neither of us wants to say them. He's a coward, but I am selfish, willful. I want to force him to break up with me because I know how hard it is for him. Breaking up with a virgin because she's a virgin. What a cad. I win. I am the more stubborn of the two.

"You're right," I nod at Chevy. I paint a grin across the width of my face and continue with my life. I go to my classes, sit on the Quad amidst Frisbee throwers and read my Great Books II texts, jotting notes in the margins of my assigned books. I go to work, put books where they belong, and organize the children's book displays, placing books with girl protagonists front and center, although there aren't that many to begin with.

I don't have a second job. After the incident with Nana at Sears, I have not returned. I am too ashamed to face my manager, to find myself in the section where I sobbed uncontrollably for all those long, unending, shuddering minutes, collecting witness after witness to name my shame. The memory of it—of that night and everything that transpired—makes me sick to my stomach, and I have to shake the thoughts and events and faces out of my head until they clear like the black eight ball whose answers disappear when it is shaken in earnest by its possessor— until it's just another blank spot of nothingness.

I enter through the automatic doors of the Queens Center Mall, across the boulevard from my apartment in Elmhurst. VIM is hiring. It's a jean store, and they hire me on the spot. They teach me to unpack boxes with new merchandise, label new clothing with price tags, and fold jeans and shirts properly on the display counters.

I meet Janipp, a skinny Puerto Rican girl with kinky black hair and a painted face. Her name is an acronym derived from the initials of both her parents' names: Juan Alexandro Nadia Isabella Pagan (her last name) Prieto (his last name)—both born-again Christians who live together in the same apartment on the other side of Queens Boulevard for financial reasons. No longer in love with each other, their mutual love for their daughter keeps them cohabitating to provide her safety and security. I trade Sheila's fading friendship and austere home for Janipp's family, which is warm and inviting.

Janipp teaches me the art of painting my face, which up until this point has been bare and real with all its flaws. She shows me how to hide not just my pimples but other parts of me—the virgin parts. We do my hair, teasing it out and fashioning it with hair spray so not even the heaviest of breezes will move it out of place. She tosses her clothes at me and pleads with me to try them on: bright red frilly shirts with low necklines, tight tank tops in blue, pink, and green that hug my breasts and ribs, my small waistline, and short spandex mini-skirts that curve around my buttocks and stick to the skin of my thighs. I wear heels for the first time, and she laughs at me when I try to find my balance.

"You look hot," she sucks her teeth at me, impressed with her artistry in taking a dowdy brown-eyed, brown-haired girl and transforming her into a beautiful girl with more curves than her jeans and loose-fitting shirts belie. We go to the mall like this, both of us dressed to the nines, and we collect phone numbers. I throw my collection in the trash, feeling uncomfortable in this new skin men's eyes find pleasure in.

"You'll get used to it," Janipp giggles at me as she places large gold hoops against my ears to see how they look. "Buy these," she orders me.

"Get used to what?" I ask her, thoughtlessly taking the hoops to the register.

"The way guys look at you," she smiles at me. "It's so hot. They can look but they can't touch."

I don't like it, but I go with it because my heart is broken and it feels like I'm getting revenge, moving on. Maybe this is part of growing up, I think, acting like a nineteen-year-old and not a twelve-year-old. This is what girls do. Express their sexuality, their desirability. For the first time, I am experimenting, and it hurts, walking around like a girl that is not me, forcing someone out of me who makes me feel like the whore my mother tells me I am.

When we get back to Janipp's home, I wash off the makeup, kick off the heels, but I leave on the mini-skirt and the tank top. This is the me I know. I can't paint myself, hide behind pink rouge and nebulous shades of eyeshadow and dark red lipstick. But I like the rest of the girl looking back at me in the mirror. I am thin, attractive, small, and curvy, and I like the way it feels not to have to hide my body anymore. I can meet Janipp in the middle, and after a few shopping treks in the mall during our breaks, I find a dark brown matte lipstick that becomes my color for the next few years—not red, not bright—just muted, like me.

Janipp takes me with her family to their church. It's a Christian church in a regular building rented out for born-again meetings. They are all Latino, and even though I am the only white person there, men, women, and kids alike welcome me. It's not like my Greek church, full of formality, Greek chanting with bearded priests dressed in long black gowns, the scent of incense smoked out of the thurible the priests swing before them as the fabric of their dress trails behind them, along aisles full of worshipers drawing a cross against their chests in response. Janipp's church is managed by her father. There is a man dressed in a navy-blue suit with a gold cross dangling against his chest hair who reads from the Bible and then talks to us as if we are his family. Then there is music, loud, Latin music, and each of us takes a tambourine, a symbol, a cowbell, and other noisemakers—there are so many to occupy our hands—and we will them to make music. Janipp and other kids begin to dance to the rhythm and beat of the bass coming from the turntable a DJ is maneuvering, and I realize that this is what family looks like—

feels like—when you can share love, friendship, and religion together with dance and music. It is pure and lovely, and I am
moved beyond words. I feel free here. Free to dance and laugh
and pray as if this were my family, my religion. I go again—many
times—not for the God they worship or the Bible stories they
share, but for the feelings that arise from the pit of my stomach
and settle into my chest whenever they begin to sing and dance.
I feel full here—the black holes inside me filled with people and
sounds of joy. I am happy here. And I know for the first time
that this is how religion should feel. Like family. Like belonging.
Like being loved.

I spend my evenings and weekends working at VIM, usually
the same shifts as Janipp, and after my shifts, I go to Janipp's
apartment only fifteen minutes away. Her parents feed me, but
mostly they leave us alone, and Janipp and I plan trips to the city,
ice-skating at the Wolman rink in the winter, Jones Beach in the
summer, double dates in between. We want to go to Cancun together when the school year is over, and I don't think about asking my mother. We take on extra shifts to pay for it.

It is still fall semester at Queens, and I spend as much time
at the student union as I can in between classes, trying to show
John he hasn't hurt me. My insides turn into a jumble of loose
jelly scraps each time I see him scouring the halls in his beige
and gray security guard's uniform. I continue to dance with my
friends on Club Night, Thursday nights, and I laugh harder than
I feel like laughing, smile wider than I feel like smiling, because I
can feel his eyes on me and my skin still burns as if nothing has
happened between us, as if we're still together, and later on that
night, I will feel his tongue press playfully past my lips and into
my mouth, hot and waiting for him. I tell myself I am over him.

Look at how much fun I am having. How happy I appear to be. How busy and forgetful I am of the last three months we spent together.

I believe it. I believe it until one day, I find myself waiting at the bus stop, and James drives past me on Kissena Boulevard. He stops the car, pulls it into reverse, pauses in front of me, and rolls down the passenger window so he can talk to me. I miss James. And Milton. I miss having a car full of friends pick me up and drive me to fun. My life is quieter now, even with Janipp by my side. Our times are girly, and I'm not all that used to a girly existence.

"What are you up to?" James yells at me over the traffic zipping past him.

"You're going to get a ticket," I laugh at him. The bus is pulling up behind him.

"I'd give you a ride, but I have to deliver these, and I'm late," he points to the bouquet of flowers in the back seat of his car—a car I used to get into when we all hung out. I don't see James anymore. Or Milton. They are John's friends.

"You work for a florist nowadays?" I joke with him.

"No, they're for . . ." And then he stops. Abruptly. As if remembering who I am for the first time in our conversation. I look at the flowers again. Beautiful. An array of pinks and reds and light blues set against a wall of green leaves, and I know they're from John. But they're not for me. Those days are over.

"I'm sorry," he sighs, pulling at the kinky curls atop his head as if punishing himself for his blunder.

"It's okay. He's moving on, right?"

"Not yet, Kath. But he's interested. She works in a doctor's office." He clamps his mouth shut as if he's said too much. He has. I don't need to know. The less I know, the better. "I gotta go. I'm so sorry."

I wave him away, unable to find the words I need to end the conversation. But as soon as his car disappears from my sight, a wail unhinges from my throat. Here I go again. What is up with all these feelings coming out of me as if they've been imprisoned and tortured and finally set free? I do not want them to be free. They make me look like a lunatic, crying at bus stops and at work and on the streets of Queens. I want to bottle them up and toss them into the toilet, where they belong.

Michelle, a friend of mine from the Jewish Club, finds me still gasping for air. Like me, she's a *shiksha*, the only other non-Jewish girl, a Catholic one with thick blond hair and crystal blue eyes who gravitated to the Jewish Club through our honors program.

"Are you alright?" She places her arms around me, and I let myself be hugged.

I laugh. "This is ridiculous," I say between gulps. "I'm crying over a guy, and I can't stop. I'm such an asshole."

She stays with me. Gets on the bus with me. Squeezes my hand when I get off the bus two stops before she does.

I call in sick at both of my jobs. I miss a week of work and a week of school. I sleep all day. My phone rings, a pink and blue pastel phone that Chevy bought for my birthday. He even paid to have it hooked to a landline, knowing that my mother would never voluntarily get me my own phone. I let the machine pick it up. Whoever it is hangs up. I don't look to see who is calling. I am huddled underneath my covers, drowsy with depression and a broken heart.

It rings again, and I ignore it again. It rings a third time, and I pick up the phone with force.

"What do you want?" I ask the offender on the other side of the line.

"Hey," John's husky voice tickles my earlobe and I remember how his lips felt against my ears.

"Why are you calling me?"

"I just want to know how you're doing. I haven't seen you, and you haven't been going to your classes."

"How do you know?" I place emphasis on you. *Why do you care?* I want to ask instead. But the less I say, the more in control I will be in this conversation.

"I just know." There is a long pause. "What are you doing right now?"

"I'm sleeping. You woke me up."

"Why are you sleeping in the middle of the day?"

His concern grates on my nerves. *Why do you think, asshole?* "What are you, my keeper?" Sarcasm is all I can muster, but my breaths are coming out fast and hard.

"Look, I just want to see if you're okay. Come back to school. I miss seeing you." That last part is soft, intended to show me he still cares.

"John," I begin, shutting my eyes and hoping I don't sound like I care. "We're not together anymore. I'm fine. But please don't call me again." I hang up the phone, angry with the little lovesick virgin inside me who wants to stay on the line, talk to him some more.

"We're over," I tell her.

"He broke up with us because we wouldn't have sex with him," I remind her.

She concedes. Begrudgingly.

The semester is a bust. I disappear from the student union. I disappear from my classes. I am taking twelve credits, but I get my first C in Biology. I opt for pass/fail in Math and Psychology, and I pass them without a letter grade. I ask for my first incomplete in Great Books II. My grades set me back a semester, and my GPA plummets. I spend my Christmas break working, saving my money for Cancun with Janipp. It's the only thing I have to look forward to, and when I am not working or hanging out with Janipp, I tuck myself between my sheet and my comforter and grind my teeth in my sleep.

Back in school in January, I see John with the new girl, a woman, really. She's older, in her twenties, full in weight and curves. She is all woman compared to my small frame and height. I am a slip of a girl next to her. She looks at me, knows who I am. Her eyes travel up and down my body, and I almost miss the slow rounded circles she makes on her belly. It takes me a second to understand the message she sends me. She is pregnant. With John's baby.

I smile. I laugh. I rejoice because I know this is not what John has in mind. He's a college kid afraid of growing up, staying in college long after he should have graduated. Now he's going to be a father, and I assume, a husband. He wants sex so bad that when he gets it, it traps him. Good job, John.

I return to my old ways. I hang out with Chevy at our regular booth and my other friends at the Jewish Club. I roam the halls of the student union, dance on Club Nights, kiss boys with laughter on my lips, and revel in the freedom I possess and he has lost. I am free of him, and just like that, I no longer pine for his kisses or the smell of him on my clothes. I catch a glimpse of his slothful strides from floor to floor and know that this is the best he will do, the most he will be. A husband and father at twenty.

I have dodged a bullet. And I know this more after the birth of his baby girl, many long months later, when our paths cross in the basement of the student union. I am walking out of the Italian Club this time, and John passes me in the hallway.

"Hey, Kath." The huskiness still resides in his voice, but it doesn't move me.

"Hey," I reply and keep walking in the opposite direction.

"That's it?" He asks, stopping me in my tracks. "Is that all I get?"

"Of course not." I turn towards him. "How's your baby girl? I hear she's very sweet."

He doesn't say anything. His mouth twists into a crooked grin as if he knows what I'm thinking. As if he's the only one in the world who knows what I am thinking. It makes me want to slap the presumptuousness from his face.

He takes a few steps towards me, and I have to step back until my spine comes up against the wall. I welcome the surface's coolness on the heated skin of my neck as I look up at John, wondering what he's up to.

He comes up against me, the buttons on his uniform grazing the cotton fabric of my thin T-shirt, and one arm locks me in place as he positions the palm of his hand against the wall, his fingers almost touching my cheek. I feel his breath fanning my eyelids, this is how close he is to me, but I can't move. I don't want to. I want to see how this will play out.

"So," he whispers, the word almost a kiss on my cheek.

"So," I arch my eyebrows at him. "What are you doing? Aren't you married?"

He ignores my question, his grin deepening. I imagine he thinks I am still in love with him, ignorant of the fact that my heart has healed, and my love for him shriveled like a dried out raisin the day I found out he would be a father.

"Are you still a virgin?" The spell he is trying to cast on me is nothing more than a grain of sand loosened and blown into the thin air that grows stale between us. I move out of his locked pose and walk away from him, leaving him with the last words I ever say to him.

"That is no longer any of your business."

THE SUN-KISSED VIRGIN

It is the summer of my twentieth birthday, and I am in Cancun, Mexico, with Janipp. I have somehow saved the money I need to pay for my flight and hotel, with barely enough saved to eat. But I don't need food. This is a basic human need but not one that takes precedence in my life. After my paychecks are put aside for tuition and the rent money I offer my mother—which she has not asked for but takes wordlessly—I have enough to buy food here and there each week. Usually, I live off Roy Rogers French fries daily. For one dollar, I can buy large fries and pick at them for the entire day—for both lunch and dinner. One Coke a day suffices for liquids people tell me I need. I am not a hungry person. Not for food. And in all honesty, I am constantly in motion from job to school to job to home with no spare time to reflect on physical needs like hunger.

I don't ask my mother if I can go to Cancun with Janipp. I just do it. Janipp's parents take us to the travel agent they know in Astoria since Janipp and I can't drive. Reliant on public transportation and without money to afford a car, it's not necessary for us to get around. We both navigate the subway system with skill we haven't acquired in other corners of our lives —like love and boys. I give my money—cash since I get paid in cash—to Janipp's father, and he puts the cost of our trip on his credit card. I am reeling in this giddy excitement flushing to my cheeks. I am going away on a trip, with a friend—not my mother. I am a seasoned traveler, but all my other journeys were guided by my mother's desires—what she wanted to see, where she wanted to travel to—freezing moments in pictures that included my face and body with a backdrop of Machu Picchu, blue-footed boobies that can only be found in the Galapagos Islands, vast electric blue oceans in which sharks are swimming between my legs, and English castles that made me love the literature and gallantry of the Middle Ages, romanticizing besotted knights without seeing the oppression their women faced.

But this is my first trip without my mother, without me chasing her feet along guided paths leading us into and out of museums and historical sites I never took an interest in. I want to go to Mexico. I want to go with my friend. I want to be free to wake up late and sunbathe all day. To go out at night and dance. To flirt with and kiss boys I will never see again. To be free, unencumbered by my mother's voice and eyes telling me what I am and who she sees in me.

When I tell her we're going to Cancun, she doesn't say anything other than, "Don't expect me to give you any money for it." I don't. I don't even ask, although I know I won't have enough left over to last the week for shopping or eating. But I don't need food. I only need my liberty, to feel a sense of myself outside of her tight-fisted mothering.

Janipp and I squeeze each other's fingers as the cab drives us to the hotel and leaves us at the entrance where a young dark-skinned man opens our doors and grabs our suitcases. We stay in a hotel that has the word Playa on it, possessing two pools, a hot tub, and a sandy trail that leads to a private sandy beach. We're led to the seventh floor, a room with a king-sized bed in the middle, a small kitchenette by the door, and a porch overlooking the crisp, light blue ocean as the backdrop of our seven-day stay. I realize that my $500 did not cover the full expense of my trip; that Janipp's father took the money I gave him but paid more with his credit card for my vacation. I kiss Janipp on the cheek, grateful for her generosity, because I know she has played a part in this. He has also opened an account for us at the hotel so we can eat and drink and make plans and put it on the tab. Despite his generosity, I try to use up my own money first, before tapping into the money he has allowed us for enjoyment. Janipp's father also gave her a camcorder, and we record everything: the beach, the pools, the two of us drinking our first piña coladas in our two-piece bikinis, her body lithe and bony and dark, and mine covered in a T-shirt that comes down to the middle of my thighs. I am still too self-conscious to expose myself, to reveal the curves that live and breathe beneath the comforting layer of my shirt, but I do take it off when I sunbathe. At night, we lie in bed, side by side, her dark brown curls and my straight brown strands becoming enmeshed as we rewind the tape to watch what we recorded from the day's events.

"Let's call ourselves by some other names." Janipp bounces on the heels of her bare feet by the pool, the hot sun beating against us with a ferocity I never felt when lying beneath the New York sun.

"Why?" I laugh at her, entering the water's surface a few feet behind her.

"It'll be so much fun. We can be someone else for the entire trip, and when we meet guys, we give them this name. What name do you want? I want to be Sam."

"I guess, Alex," I reveal after a few minutes of silence. "I just love that it can be a guy's name or a girl's name."

"Okay, Alex. Don't slip with my name. I'm Sam from now on," she laughs, casting me a warning look from above her round sunglasses. "*Dos mojitos, por favor,*" she orders for us when a waiter passes us. I envy Janipp's confidence. The way she carries herself, her shoulders straight, her eyes always flirtatious and laughing. She is aware of her beauty, her charm, and she uses these with a skill I have not mastered or even attempted to master.

When I walk into a room, I am only aware of myself, my unsteady footing, wondering where I can sit or stand without bringing any attention to myself. I look for corners in which to hide, hoping no one sees me and talks to me because they think I want to be spoken to. I don't. I like to sit on the outskirts of scenes and watch people, make up stories about them in my head, and examine the movements of their limbs showing me who they are beneath painted faces and grinning mouths. Being with Janipp forces me into the center of conversations and circles instead of at the edge of them where I feel most at home. She commands attention and has no problem giggling or eyeing boys for it. Although everything about her is rooted in the dark Puerto-Rican tones of her heritage, she covers her chocolate brown eyes with blue contact lenses that peer out of a brown face haloed by even darker hair. The difference is stark, but gorgeous, and I realize how blue eyes alone have the power to invite the attention of the opposite sex.

I close my eyes against the visual scene of her flirtations and bathe my skin in the hot glow of the sun beams, feeling the rays enter my pores and slide beneath my skin, like golden hands sprawled all over me, spanning my body, caressing every inch of me that is seen and unseen. Sun-bathing feels like making love. The sun is an all-consuming lover rendering me submissive as he overtakes me from above, and I feel my hips rise and open slightly, welcoming his force, his vigor, taking him into me, feeling the energy of his every fiber kissing my skin, fluttery sensations surging in my abdomen, multiplying, struggling against each other for release. It is a sweet and sensual experience, and there has been no other that has made me want to submit, to give in, to open up to its natural pleasures.

"Kathy!" I hear Janipp's heavy whisper pulling me out of my tryst with the sun. "Let's go in the pool. There are some cute guys there." She points to three boys in their late teens.

"Janipp, they're babies," I point out to her, but she only laughs.

"C'mon." She rises from her lounge chair and pulls me by my fingers, dragging me behind her.

Two of the boys, Horacio and Juan, are brothers. Esteban, the chubby one, is their cousin. The five of us are in the pool, forming a circle, and they invite us to play volleyball, even though there is no net between us. Janipp introduces us as Sam and Alex, and I let it go for now, trying to remember to turn my head when one of them calls me by my phony name.

I can tell Janipp has her eyes set on Juan, the sixteen-year-old, and, as they form a team, I am left with Esteban and Horacio on the other side. Horacio is eighteen and breathtaking to look at. He is tall and thin and dark, but his shoulder-length and loose black curls fall into his rich, brown eyes and it's like watching poetry assembling right in front of me without words. He's lovely to look at, but I talk more to Esteban, because I know Horacio is out of my league. I am twenty, too old for him, short, and I still cover myself in a loose T-shirt that only shows off my legs —muscular, thin, and tanned. I am not a woman. Just a girl. A plain and ordinary girl without any game or wiles.

The boys all live in a suburban part of Mexico City, but they have come to Cancun with their father and grandmother for summer vacation. Horacio and Juan's parents are divorced, so this is their father's gift to them. Esteban is there to watch over them, to make sure they're not seduced into sex or drugs or alcohol by strangers. They stay in the part of the hotel for wealthy people, sleeping in an apartment-style suite with a living room, a full kitchen, and three bedrooms. We meet the boys' father, a serious middle-aged man who looks very much like both his sons in height and features, and he invites us to go snorkeling. Janipp consents before I can say anything.

"Are you crazy?" I turn to her afterwards. "We don't know them. We're two girls in a foreign country. We can't just go off with people in their cars without knowing them."

"Kath, they're a family. A dad with his two sons and a nephew. Going snorkeling. Nothing's going to happen."

Sometimes I wonder about Janipp. She is too trusting. Growing up in New York, you learn not to trust, to stare at empty spaces between a cluster of people, but to be aware of everyone's movements at the same time. You can never be caught off your guard, and yes, we are on vacation, but this is when it's most dangerous. At least for girls, young girls in a party city among multitudes of partiers.

"We'll be fine," she sticks her tongue out at me. "We're together. I got your back."

I grunt my consent.

Horacio's father picks us all up in his minivan, and I am squeezed between Esteban and Horacio in the middle of the van with Janipp and Juan taking the seats all the way in the back. Once we enter the water park, Horacio's father pays for our tickets. I try to give him my money, not wanting this stranger, as generous as he is, to pay for all of us. But he won't take it. When he goes to pay for lunch, the same struggle ensues, me offering him my money, and him refusing to let me pay.

"Your money is no good here," he tells me with perfect but accented English. "You and your friend are my guests."

It's true that I don't have a lot of money with me, but it is such an uncomfortable situation to have someone else, a stranger, pay for me. Janipp doesn't have a problem with this. She keeps giving me the "shut up" glare she likes to give me when all the rules in my head get in the way of our fun—face pointed at me, eyes wide and rounded, lips pursed into a tight and wrinkled line—but I just give it right back at her with a shake of my head.

I don't win with their father, and every time I offer him my money, he smiles and shakes his head. When we get back to the hotel, I thank him profusely, in English and in the limited Spanish I know, and shake his hand. When I turn to leave, I bump into Horacio's solid chest and catch him smiling at me and then over my head at his father. I blush but wave good-bye and follow Janipp towards our room.

The next day, Janipp and I walk to the mall a few blocks from our hotel for lunch and order chicken sandwiches, fries, and soft drinks from McDonald's. As I make my way to the table with my tray, a young man bumps into me, spilling his soda all over the floor with its ice and sticky sweet substance spraying my flip flops and ankles. His friends, all older, in their mid-twenties, a few feet away from me, laugh aloud at him, forcing his cheeks to take on a pink hue beneath his tanned face.

"I'm so sorry," he yelps, running to get napkins and then giving them to me to wipe my feet. I put my own tray down at the nearest table, wipe the dregs of his drink off my toes, and smile up at him.

"It's okay," I laugh. "It was an accident. No harm done."

He whispers his apology to me one more time and then walks over to his friends, all of them looking over at me and Janipp. One pair of sea-green eyes catches my attention and only because he keeps looking at me as if there is some mystery to be solved in the quiet movements of my limbs. I ignore him but am hyper aware of his eyes following me the entire hour I sit with my back to him, talking to Janipp, pretending not to feel him on me.

Janipp's eyes focus on a sudden movement over my head, and I follow her gaze, turning slightly in my chair. I find those eyes, right there, so near me, smiling down at me.

"Hi, I'm John."

God. Another John.

"I'm Sam," Janipp pipes up. "And this is Alex."

"I'm Kathy," I correct her, no longer wanting to play this juvenile game that posits me as a liar.

His gaze is warm as it rests on me, and his smile widens. "Kathy. So, who's Alex?"

"No one. Just an inside joke." My hands reach for my Coke and I take a sip from the straw, relieved to feel the cool liquid inside my already dry mouth and throat. Every inch of me is wondering why this guy is talking to me.

And he is talking to me. Looking at me. Smiling at me. Not

at Janipp. Me. He's tall and solid, not long and scrawny like Horacio. My hands want to reach out and squeeze the muscles that push against the black fabric of his T-shirt as it curves around his biceps, his stomach, even his shoulders. He is well-built and beautiful to look at. Sexy is a better word, with his green eyes laughing at me with curiosity while winding his tapered fingers through his short but wavy dark-brown hair.

"Kathy." He says again, rolling the sound of my name on his tongue as if to taste it. "I don't know if you're interested, but my friends and I are going to a club tonight, and we'd love it if you and your friend joined us. It's called the Luna. We'll be there around nine thirty."

"That sounds great," Janipp pipes up, assuming my voice for me, although not exactly my words.

"I hope I see you there," he places his hand on my shoulder, and I feel its heat transfer into me, leaving a tingling sensation behind when he pulls it away as if he is already missed, an absence that needs to be filled.

"Holy shit, he's hot!" Janipp whispers heavily into the air between us when he is out of earshot. "We have to go."

"Do we?" I whine a little bit. "He's too much for me. Horacio's more my speed, no?"

"Horacio's a boy. This guy, John, he's a man." She waves her fingers in her face as if to cool herself in that melodramatic way of hers that makes me giggle. "And he's into you. Oh my God, he was staring at you the whole time. Ever since his friend spilled his drink on you."

"But I'm not ready for a man, Janipp." I sigh, taking another slow sip from my drink. "I'm not ready for any of it."

"Kath," Janipp reaches over to shake my shoulder with her

red manicured nails. "You're in Cancun. What happens in Cancun, stays in Cancun. Just have fun. You can do whatever you want. No one's here to tell you anything else or to judge you. Enjoy yourself. Be free." With that, she closes her eyes, lifts her head and hands to the air above her, and starts to hum Madonna's "Like a Virgin."

"Shut up!" I laugh at her.

"Let's go shopping for tonight," Janipp moves quickly out of her seat and grabs my hand, and we are off before I can protest that I have enough clothes and don't need any more. But I follow her with a mix of anxiety and excitement—a drink of opposites sure to entice any virgin into easy submission.

Hours later, we enter the threshold of the Luna, a club full of young, drunk tourists from the neighboring hotels bouncing in unison to the loud, deep bass of house music intended to make bodies jolt into one another like electricity, all endowed with a paid stamp on one hand and a glass of fruity colored alcohol draped around ice cubes in another. My legs and hips adopt the rhythm of the music, and Janipp and I advance towards the bar together, becoming enmeshed in the tangled wave of bodies stirring like graceful notes in a melody that absorbs us.

Janipp orders Sex on the Beach, because we like the sweet taste of the drink and because she likes to scream out the name of it for attention, agreeing over the loud music that we will not take drinks from anyone. We buy our own drinks, and we don't leave them unattended. This is for two reasons: one, so we don't feel like we owe guys anything for buying us a drink, and two, because we want to make sure no guy drugs us so he can have his way with us. If we end up with a guy, it's because we want to, not because we're too drunk to know better or too drunk to be present. We also agree on one drink for the night, and that is all. We're both small and thin, so alcohol, when it hits us, hits us hard. One Sex on the Beach numbs my chin and loosens my inhibitions enough so that I can enjoy the vibrations of the music on my skin and in my bones. I can close my eyes and dance like a wild girl who laughs more than she thinks.

When I open my eyes, my gaze is enfolded within the grasp of a deep shade of green that feels like home, like love waiting for me. My body continues to sway to the beat of the song whose name I don't know or care, and I watch John make his way to me without breaking the trance. What is this attraction between two strangers that requires no words, no language, nothing more than a look, a smile? It's so becoming, so seductive and electric. When he reaches me, his hands wrap around my waist, and we move into each other, not in that gross, sweaty way surrounding us—bodies grinding against each other with force and lust, pornography and alcohol blindly mixed together—but in the sweet and gentle way of strangers who like each other coming together for the first time. There is curiosity in our touches, a questioning of boundaries and permissions, his fingers winding their way to the small of my back, his body swaying with mine, a small space of charged currents amassing between us with the desire for contact to close the gap. I am dizzy now, crumbling into him, my feet getting tangled in his, and he takes hold of my fingers and leads me to a quiet corner, away from the dancers and the noise.

"Do you want a drink?"

I shake my head, so heavy now on my shoulders. "Just water, please."

He leaves me and I take a deep breath, trying to calm my pulse from racing against my throat. He returns with a bottle of water, places it against my cheek, smiling when I gasp with pleasure at its coolness, and opens it for me. I take a sip, release a long, happy sigh, and lean my back against the wall to steady me. He is so close I can smell the crisp scent of his cologne intermingled with sweat and the strong desire to run my fingers along the muscular contours of his chest as they protrude from his pale blue T-shirt expanding with each melodic note of music around us that matches my pulse racing beneath my skin.

I offer him my water instead and watch his smile disappear when he takes a swig from the opening. It returns, his teeth white and straight as they form into a grin that makes his eyes twinkle with humor.

"You're beautiful," he breaks my trance with his words. I feel my face flush with heat, and I wonder what it is these boys seem to find in me that they call me beautiful. It's not a word I would use to describe myself. Beautiful makes me suspicious, as if they know that if they call us this word that only describes two percent of the population, we will be more inclined to have sex with them. But I hear Janipp's voice in my head telling me to accept a compliment, so I say nothing.

"You're pretty beautiful yourself," I tell him, grinning back. And he is. Striking. So much so that I begin to scour the crowd of dancers for girls he should be hitting on instead of me. I find her. She is tall and thin with a one-piece black spandex dress hugging her small breasts and stretching against the protruding hip bones of her flat midsection. She has dark brown hair and when she looks in our direction, I find a matching set of eyes. *How can two girls with similar features look so different*, I think quietly, unaware that John is looking at me, taking it all in. This is the girl he should be flirting with, not me.

"You can look like that if you wanted," his voice breaks into my negative thoughts, and I blush with shame. "But I think you're beautiful as you are, right now, without the tight dress and the high heels she can't dance in or the makeup that hides her real face. You're pretty without any of that crap."

"How do you know what I'm thinking?" I ask him, the alcohol having seeped out of my pores, making me aware and awake for the first time since I arrived.

"Because I'm watching you, and everything is in your face. You don't hide much," he smiles again as if he sees something else in me I don't want him to see.

"Really?" I roll my eyes at him. "What am I thinking right now?"

"I think you want me." He pauses, turning that smile I want to touch with my fingertips towards the crowd before us. "You want me to dance with you," he finishes his sentence and pulls my hand onto his shoulder, where I can feel the tense muscles of his back stiffen at my touch, and I know he wants me, too. Although what good all this wanting will do us, I don't know. But for now, for this one moment, we can dance, letting the music enfold us into the crowd that clumsily pushes us into each other, currents of energy charging and emitting sexual wantonness from one desirous form to another. It's all there, around us, forces beyond my understanding, but I push it all inside, wanting nothing more than to dance with him. I hope for a later, when we are all alone and I can brush my lips across his to taste the way he makes me feel when he looks at me, like a drop of thick honey on my tongue.

It is two in the morning when we leave the club. John and I walk behind Janipp and his friends, together, our fingers clasped, our legs and shoulders bumping into each other, prolonging the heady sensations that stir and warm and arouse when we connect, pull away, and then connect again. Janipp and his friends decide to go night swimming, and John and I follow them to the outdoor pool of their hotel. I laugh when Janipp throws herself into the pool with her clothes on, John's friends hollering as they follow suit, three sets of cannonballs crashing through the surface, all fully clothed.

John pulls me against his side, slips his arm around my shoulders, and I can hardly breathe, the tension between us so thick and sweet that I am ready to kiss him. More than ready.

"Do you want to go up to my room?" he asks, the huskiness in his voice a warning to me.

"I do," I tell him, so hungry for just one taste of him that I am reeling in blindness, hardly able to catch my breath or focus my eyes on him. "But I have to tell you. I won't have sex with you. I want to kiss you, but not sex. I just met you. I like you, but no to that."

"It's okay. No sex. I just want to lie next to you. Is that okay?"

My response comes out weak, but I nod my head like a child who has lost all capacity for speech. I follow him, praying he doesn't turn out to be a handsy dick. That he doesn't ruin my fantasy of him, the pure and beautiful feelings meeting him has heightened in me.

My heart is thrashing against my ribcage when we enter his room and he closes the door behind us. I know this is dangerous, that it upsets all my self-determined expectations for remaining a virgin, but I trust him. I know that nothing more than what I want to happen will happen. Because I like him, I want him, but I don't love him. I want to explore these feelings, this sexual tension that moves me beyond verbal expression, because it is so new to me. I am an explorer, a student. I am clear, burdened only by this deep-seated burning desire I have to kiss him. To be kissed by him. To find myself tangled in his arms with a want that has no words or boundaries except the ones I assign it.

"I just want to lie beside you," he says again, pulling me onto the bed in the middle of the room, the sheer curtains by the open glass doors that overlook the expansive ocean set against dark skies and the hotel's pool swishing and stirring with the rhythm of the breeze from the salty night air playing against its soft, fluttery fabric. Entranced by it, I let him pull me down on the bed, and we lie there, facing each other, in fetal positions, our knees bent and touching. John reaches his right hand over and pushes a strand of hair away from my eyes, half-closed from fatigue and need intermingled. My lips part as if to signal my request, and in response, his face comes closer to mine. I hold on to his eyes as if pulling him to me by an invisible cord connecting us, and when his lips brush against mine for the first time, it is everything I expect and want. It is gentle and hard, fire and ice, patient and hungry—all at the same time, a ball of heat growing in the pit of my belly and rising to my chest, then my throat, then the mouth that welcomes his tongue, his breath into mine. I am sated. And he seems to be, too. He does not climb on top of me as the old John did, or slide his hands up my shirt, or pull my fingers onto the bulge I know is growing between us. He stays on his fetal side, and I remain on mine, the only parts of us touching, our knees, our hands—his cupping my chin to angle my mouth deeper into his, mine resting on the fabric of his shoulder and then meandering into the waves of his dark hair, untangling the gel that keeps it smooth and sleek. I press the back of his head closer to mine as if we can get deeper into each other, our mouths and lips and tongues more intimate, more central to the core of our needs.

When we can kiss no more, we pull apart, knees still scraping against knees, fingers intertwined, eyes clasped as if in an embrace neither one of us wants to tear apart from.

"I see you, you know," he murmurs in my ear, the hairs inside tingling for more of his sweet, cool breath to call to them again.

"And what is it that you see?" I arch my eyebrows at him, expecting a typical boy-hitting-on-girl response, a bit amused, but more alarmed he will turn out to be just another boy trying to get to my sex with words he thinks will disarm me.

"You're good and kind. It's what woke me up to you at the mall. When Trey spilled his drink on you, I expected you to scream at him, throw your drink in his face. Most girls I know would have. But you didn't. You laughed instead. You were kind to him. You didn't care about getting soda on your clothes or shoes. You were just so cool about it."

"Really?" I laugh. "That's all? That's nothing. It's ridiculous to get pissed off at that. It was obviously an accident."

"No, most girls would have reacted differently. That's when I knew I had to talk to you, get to know you. You surprise me. And no one surprises me anymore."

There is a sadness to his tone that beckons me to caress him with my eyes, drink in his sweetness, and then reach my forefinger out to touch the dimple that widens when he smiles. He is smiling right now, and I want to kiss him again, memorize the parts of him that will disappear when morning sneaks in to rouse us from this frozen moment.

"You surprise me, too." I let out a long, slow sigh and sink into the pillow that cushions my head.

I know him. I have known him forever. I don't say this to him, but I don't think I need to. I know he feels the same way. I also know I will never see him again, even though he lives in Long Island, forty minutes from my home in Queens. Even though he gives me his number and address, I know this will be our only time together. I won't call him. I won't see him. Because if I do, I will want to do more with him, to know more of him, of his hands, his tongue, the muscled contours of his body and how they would feel if I released them from the fabric of his clothes. I would love him beyond words and flirting and fetal positions that keep us at bay from the intimacy we both seem to crave and control at the same time. I want this moment to last forever and know that it will only remain this perfect, this flawless, here and now, if I leave it here and now. It will die in the future, in New York, where the gray scales of the city and its ragged realities will claw at the luster and innocence and make it as the city is—as love seems to be—aged and common and full of impurities. It's what happened with Ray, and I don't want to ruin this. I want to stay here, lying beside him, locked in his gaze, on the covers of a bed in the middle of a room in Mexico, where we are perfect and perfectly in sync. Where we are new to each other and our flaws have not yet presented themselves and become entangled and rusty with time, like barbed wire fences that keep you in with fear and tear your flesh when you try to escape its confines. That's what love ends up being: barbed wire that traps and tears and hurts.

After John falls asleep, I kiss him lightly on the lips, a last taste that is insufficient and leaves an ache in my gut, and I exit his room without sharing my address or my phone number back home. I find Janipp asleep by the pool, still wet and fully clothed, a towel draped over her to keep her warm, a row of boys snoring on lounge chairs beside her. I wake her, hold her drowsy head up with my shoulder, and grab a cab to our own hotel, my thoughts still swooning with John, the feel and smell of him a resonating echo on my flesh.

WHEN TWO VIRGINS COLLIDE

Back at the hotel, there is Horacio—tall, lanky, and young, his curls swirling across his questioning eyes. When the short burst of a hot breeze sweeps over our sunbathed bodies by the poolside, I am surprised to find him looking at me. He lacks the husky masculinity of John that appeals to me, but his innocence reels me in with unintended precision.

He is a virgin. I know because his hands never skulk around my body when we're playing volleyball in the pool. He holds my hand and smiles at me, but there is no lust there, lurking in his limbs or his eyes when they pull me to him. Part of me holds back because of John. I can still feel his mouth on mine, his hands in my hair, and I want to run back to the hotel and the bed we shared for nothing more than one last long, lazy look at him. But I stay rooted to my lounge chair, follow Horacio and Janipp and Juan and Esteban without thinking into the pool, into the cafe, back to the lounge chairs, back to the beach where we jump the crisp green waves that collide with our bodies, pushing us up against each other, sleek skin bathed in salty water and sun. I am not present, my shoulders limp, and I ignore Horacio's gaze when he asks me if I'm alright.

He thinks I am jealous because Juan and Janipp are fooling around, making out in the water while we sit on the sand looking out into the clear blue skies above them. He thinks I want a romantic interlude for myself, but I don't tell him about John, about the emptiness that has made a comfortable home in me, the weeping, starving girl who screams and claws along my insides trying to escape.

"I'm not jealous," I tell him. "It's great that they're having a good time."

"I like you." He lowers his voice into a whisper so that Esteban does not hear.

"I like you, too," I turn my head to him, clasping my knees to my chest, and smiling at him.

"No, I like you. A lot. Like that," he nods his head towards Janipp and Juan, their bodies intertwined, mouths attached, waves lapping against their shoulders and splashing their faces as they kiss.

"Oh," I blush, hoping the flush I feel generating in my cheeks doesn't show from beneath my tan.

I am dark, almost as dark as Horacio, except his color is rich brown-black and mine is golden. My Greek roots never burn from the sun's rays—they only go dark, beautiful, deep. Like Horacio.

He reaches out to hold my hand, running his fingers over mine, outlining the unmanicured and chewed fingernails with his own long and tapered ones.

I spend the remaining days of my trip with him, walking along the beach with the foam of the ocean's water teasing our toes, submerging our feet with warm liquid that covers our footprints as we stroll past. We hold hands, fingers interlocked, his tall form gently pressing into mine when he looms over me for a kiss. His kiss is not John's. It's soft and gentle but lacks that intensity, that fathomless, gaping need John's kisses left in me, like feeding a starving child. No matter how much John gave, I wanted more. Perhaps this is better—not wanting, not needing with such immeasurable desire that leaves me unsated. Soft, gentle kisses that probe and pause and taste out of curiosity and not hunger is a sweet, cathartic kind of kiss intended to heal the pain that comes with loss, with absence. Horacio's kisses heal me from John's all-consuming, chasmic ones that left me trembling for hard objects to hold on to. When two virgins collide, the energy forms a light, thin spark, not a yawning, ceaseless electrical fire that cannot be controlled. I prefer the slow, the controlled, the tempered love that doesn't challenge me for more—to give up the parts of me that want to remain untouched and unsoiled.

I like kissing a virgin. Knowing his experience ends with kissing, his hands pinned to my waist, my ribcage, never daring to go past the barriers outlined for him by my clothing and his inexperience. We are on equal footing, and he won't ask for more because he doesn't know more. When we go for walks along the water's edge at night, it also helps that his cousin goes with us, acting like a chaperone who won't leave our side. He lies on the sand while Horacio and I walk towards the water snaking its way up to the sand and circling our toes. He sits on the lounge chairs by the pool when Horacio and I decide to go night swimming, arms wound around the other's neck in a long kiss, chlorine-packed waves lapping against our shoulders and backs, the swishing motion pushing and pulling us against each other with the rhythm and cadence of a child's lullaby.

I am safe with Horacio. Safe and warm and protected, his virginity a sure and comfortable escape from the realities of ceaseless passion that have one direct path to sex. I start to believe I should only date virgins, but I wonder how many virgins I will find in their twenties. Especially boy virgins. They seem to lose their virginity in high school as if they are in a race against time, the last virgin being cast a loser in life and social circles of coolness and status. Horacio is a virgin only because he is still young, eighteen, and I wonder if he thinks I will teach him the ropes, take it from him as if it is a disease that needs a cure. I will not be his teacher. I have nothing to teach him, except the value of a long, deep kiss that keeps me by his side, wanting nothing more than to be enveloped by his quietude, his tenderness, feeling tender myself while in his arms. Perhaps it is this tenderness that makes me panic and look elsewhere for the dangers his loving attention is lacking.

The night before we leave, Janipp and I go to a Booze Cruise, a favorite pastime for tourists who can get as blitzed as they want on a boat, in the middle of the ocean, captains and servers navigating their drunken bodies on and off the boat, from bar to bar and from drink to drink. This time, I get drunk. Like big time drunk. So drunk, I have to lie down on the ground to hold me up because I am too tired to move, too dizzy to stand. I have a variety of drinks—beer, Sex on the Beach, but Long Island Iced Tea is what bends me over the edge.

I begin with a Corona that Janipp places in my hand, a free drink from Andrew and Dave, two boys our age that Janipp meets on the dance floor while I am leaning my head over the edge of the moving ship, my eyes shut to the onslaught of the wind racing against my face. Janipp has her eyes on Andrew, an Italian college guy from the Bronx. He is chubby and dark-haired, and Janipp is giddy with flirtation for him. Dave is thin, but not Horacio-thin, with a full head of gold-blonde hair and eyes that reflect the ocean's gleaming green-blue hues. They are like staring into crystals, fathomless and startling. He is Cuban, and he and Andrew have been best friends since elementary school. Dave and I are left talking to each other as Janipp and Andrew find corners to sink into, kissing heavily and openly, but I am hardly there, wishing I was feeling the grainy sand shift beneath my feet with Horacio's breath fanning my eyelashes closed while he leans into me for a kiss.

By my third drink, the Long Island Iced Tea, which I have never had before, I am tripping over my own feet, and Janipp rushes over to guide me to a seat.

"Andrew says he's into you," she giggles when she draws my shoulders towards her and I can meet her gaze without wavering.

"Who? Andrew?" My voice squeaks, my drunken breath assaulting her nostrils, her head inching away from me, her eyes, two bright blue twinkling stars laughing at me.

"No, stupid! Dave! Kiss him. We can end up dating two best friends. We're best friends. They're best friends. Think of all the double dates we can have together. Kiss him," she hisses into my neck and leaves me there to consider her grand idea. I burst into laughter, and Dave sits next to me, grinning at my giddiness. I am a different girl now. I have no inhibitions. My body is not held together with the glue of my virtues, and my mind is reeling with easy chuckling that comes from nowhere and ends up pushing my body forward in a string of hiccups. This makes me laugh more, and Dave watches me with humor, taking it upon himself to guard me while Janipp disappears into the shadows again with Andrew.

"I think they're making out again," I snigger at Dave.

"Probably," he nods his head at me. "You want to join them?"

"Sure," I laugh again. "Why the hell—" He interrupts my response by leaning into me and placing his mouth on mine, his tongue entering the wall of my lips without hesitation. He pulls away, his eyes seeking mine for approval, and I lean my head back against the headrest and smile at him. *Go ahead*, I think to him. *Kiss me again.*

But Dave is not John. And he is not Horacio. I am not Kathy to him. He doesn't know Kathy like they do, and he doesn't care about Kathy. She is just a girl to him. A drunk girl with breasts to cup, a vagina to rub against, and skin to trail hands over. I know who he is. I've seen him before, met him before, kissed him before, fought against his ravenous hands before.

But I let him kiss me, because my heart is soft and tender at the loss of the first John, and the second John, and Horacio— who I wish I was with right now, back at the hotel—not here, in the middle of the ocean, on a booze cruise with a Cuban boy who has sex written all over him, the letters of his desire dancing with excitement in deep sea-green eyes so wondrous to look at and easy to disappear into.

I am not the girl I am with Horacio, the sensible virgin, and I am not the girl I was with the second John, the deep, thoughtful, loving girl. I am the drunk girl with Dave. The one who lets him guide her into a shadowy corner against the boat's bow, his tongue darting in and out of my mouth, his fingers sneaking underneath my tank top, underneath my bra, until they find my nipples and squeeze, forcing my body to pulse and vibrate, my own hands gripping the muscles of his back, pressing my hips into his as if he were my old John, my first John. I am the girl who wants him to kiss all the gaping wounds and losses in me with blind sex, with unembodied hands and lips belonging to a stranger I don't care about and don't crave to see again. I am the girl I don't like to see in the mirror the next morning, avoiding the shame I know I will find there glaring back at me, the disappointment that poisons my stomach with the memory of his hands on my bare skin, my own lustful response when I grind my hips into his to feel the bulge between my thighs, even while fully clothed, my legs shaking with want I could satisfy with Dave or any other stupid boy who expects sex from a drunk girl he just met.

But I'm not stupid. Drunk or not, I am still me, still a virgin, and I don't let a moment of weakness, of lust, rob me of my own desires. I will wait for love. I will wait for patience. I will wait for a boy who knows me and accepts all of me, not just my breasts and thighs and the target of their single-minded invasion that rests between those thighs, irrespective of the girl attached to them.

Dave is not the kind of boy who will wait for a girl like me, love a girl like me, but I will take from him what I want just like he takes from me what he wants. I have fun. I laugh. I'm drunk. I'm free. His roving hands feel good against my skin, and I feel relieved when they don't roam farther than my hips, the curve of my butt when he pushes me against his own swollen thighs. We reach my limit wordlessly, and he breathes into my mouth, "It's okay. No rush." I whisper back into his, "Okay," and we continue the cavernous exploration of tongue and mouth and ceaseless cravings until the boat docks and we are ushered into the folds of a drunken crowd towards the exit ramps.

The next day, we have an evening flight back to New York. Janipp and I pack and place our bags behind the concierge desk. We go to the pool for a last dip and to spend our time with the boys we have grown to care for. Despite my actions the night before with Dave, my heart hankers for Horacio, who has grown on me, and I wish I could take him home with me, see him after our trip ends. It is a bitter-sweet feeling to sit with him, touch him, knowing that this will be the last time I ever see him. He and I spend our last hours by the pool. He is in the water and I want to join him, but I don't want to get wet before my flight—and I don't have my bathing suit on. I sit at the edge of the pool instead, my legs wide open, feet submerged in the water, and he stands in front of me, his body squeezed between my thighs. I keep him close to me, tight against me, his head bent towards mine, holding on to him, the feel of his skin against me warm and safe, afraid that as soon as I let go, I will lose him forever.

It is at this point that Andrew and Dave walk towards the pool. They have decided to surprise us before we leave. My arms still wrapped around Horacio, I look over his head at Dave, and our eyes meet. I smile, a slow blush of pink scouring my cheeks, but I don't let go of Horacio. Dave is Dave. Horacio is Horacio. And my heart loves Horacio, my body clings to his without the shame or repulsion that Dave engendered in me the night before, and although I don't want to hurt Dave, I don't move away from Horacio. I wave to them and point to where Janipp is lying on a lounge chair with a fruity drink in her hands on the far end of the pool, her sunglasses sheltering her from the sun's assault.

"Who are they?" Horacio turns his body towards me, my arms still encircled around his neck, and he rests his chin on my shoulder, breathing slowly against my cheek.

"These guys we met last night. Janipp has a thing for the dark-haired one. I guess he came to surprise her." It's half a lie. A lie by omission.

"You should go over. They're trying to get your attention," he looks over at the trio and nods his head at them.

"I don't want to leave you." I tell him.

"I'll be right here when you come back." He kisses me on the lips softly, and I want to curl into him, pull him over me like a blanket and freeze time altogether.

"Okay," I say and pull away against my will, rise to my feet and walk towards the lazy green-blue specks swallowing me.

"Hey," Dave says. "So, who's that? Your boyfriend." The last part is not a question. It's a statement.

"I'm sorry," I tell him. "Not a boyfriend exactly, since I've only known him for a few days. But he's someone I care about."

"I get it." He grins at me, and I suddenly feel his fingers burning my skin even though he doesn't touch me. "You're on vacation. You're having a good time."

"I really like you. I do," I tell him, sensing Janipp and Andrew move away enough to give us privacy. "I had a nice time last night."

"But." He articulates the qualifier missing from my sentence but still lurking there, standing solid and bold between us. "Listen, go. I understand. I hope I can call you when we get back to New York. I'm minutes from you, and I'd like to see you."

"Yeah, sure. Sounds like fun. I'll see you later," I tell him, feeling Horacio's eyes on us, my skin prickling with the pull of him, like going back to him is where home is. Where love lives.

I walk back to my spot on the pool ground and take Horacio into me. We sit there, my legs draped around his hips, my arms touching the wet skin of his arms and shoulders, our heads touching at the forehead, not saying anything with words, but speaking volumes with our need to touch and hold each other, not letting go until we absolutely have to. Until Horacio's father approaches us with an offer to drive us to the airport, his mere presence forcing us apart, the sudden separation feeling like a loss I'm not quite ready for, an emptiness I know I will never fill with another boy, another experience like this one—two virgins colliding and falling in love from the opposite ends of the world.

I decline the offer, telling him we already paid for a taxi to pick us up. Another lie. He shakes my hand, which I have to pull away from Horacio's to shake, and says he hopes to see me again.

"I want nothing more," I tell him, my eyes traveling from his to his son's, and I miss Horacio already.

After he leaves the pool area, Horacio and I make our way to the front desk, inside the hotel, where Janipp and I need to grab our bags and catch our ride. Andrew wants to take us to the airport, too, but Dave would also be with us. I tell him no, having to pull Janipp aside to explain to her that I can't get into a cab with two guys while Horacio is watching me leave. Janipp stomps her foot against the linoleum floor of the hotel and hugs Andrew, whispering in his ear. They will see each other when we get home. I will never see Horacio again. He will be like a dream. So today, I am selfish. I get my way, and I don't care about the wants of anyone else.

Andrew and Dave say their goodbyes, get into a taxi, and leave. This frees me to leave Horacio unencumbered by guilt and shame for being with someone other than him.

He hugs me tightly, places a piece of paper with his address and phone number in the palm of my hand, kisses me softly on the lips.

"I love you, Kathy." He cups my chin and says the words with his eyes looking into mine, so that the message has no way of getting lost or disappearing from the space that exists between us and the wider space that will come later, after I get into the cab, go to the airport, and board a plane for a home that is nowhere near his own. A home that will feel strange and cold and barren without him in it.

"I love you, too," I whisper back, choking back tears I never expected to begin in my chest and snowball into my throat.

Leaving Mexico, leaving Horacio, feels like I am leaving my heart behind. There is no love like virgin love, like Horacio love. Earnest, pure, kind, and wholly enveloping. This kind of love is hard to find, if you find it at all. It is the love I have searched for and found by accident, without knowing how much it is needed until it is left behind and lost forever. But this is the love I want, I have been searching for. One without conditions and force and pressure to do more than love. Simple and quietly abiding love in its purest form.

Having found its existence, going back home, I know what I am now looking for and the kind of guy who will give it to me.

THE SACRIFICE OF VIRGINS

During our trip, Janipp and I signed up for a tour of the Chichén Itzá Mayan ruins. I remember standing at the edge of the cenotes, looking into the depths of water-filled sinkhole caves in which the ancient Mayans used to toss the small bodies of their children to appease the rain god, Chaac. They chose children between the ages of three and eleven because they were the most innocent, untarnished by corruption and life experience. Children were sacrificed because of their purity. They were still virgins. It was an act of reverence, for the gods only desired pure sacrifices, according to the sacrificers. The good are sacrificed for the bad, the undeserving, whether it's for droughts or famines. The bad aren't tossed into the natural wells and drowned, their bodies dismembered first—the good ones are— the ones we should be honoring and loving instead. Children killed before they could live. Children killed by their community, by their own parents.

A twenty-year-old virgin holding onto the strands of my own innocence as if it is my only lifeline, I recall feeling uneasy by the site of sacrifice for people like me. The irony does not fail to make me stand up straighter, pushing my already burdened shoulders up and back, a solid wall holding up my chest. I try to keep a clean life, to keep myself clean and unsullied, so I can look at my reflection in mirrors without shame or regret, but no one else sees this as honor or as a virtue. They see it only as a hindrance to their pleasure or as a judgment. It is neither. It's for me. My virginity is mine. This is how I want to be, for me. Not for religious reasons. Not for political reasons. But for Kathy reasons. For me reasons that allow me to keep my shoulders straight and proud. And when I return to New York, this is what I face: Disgrace. Sacrifice. Rejection for abstaining from the one thing that will erase my difference and make me like everyone else.

Before I left for Cancun, I was seeing a boy I called Boo. Boo is not his name, of course. His name is Michael, but he calls me Boo, so I call him Boo back.

I meet him through my friend Diane and her boyfriend Jacob.

Diane is a pale, dark-haired Jewish girl I meet in my psychology class at Queens College. She's studying social work and wants to help children find homes to shelter them and people to love them. Her parents are well-off, but they live in Westchester. Diane attended all-Black and Latin-American schools where she was one of the few white kids among them. She is a white girl who dances to hip hop and swishes her head in circles when she's angry. When we go dancing, we do hip-hop together, but where my movements are all girly and swirly, hers are tough and gritty— what she has learned from going to a school where she's always on her guard and has to be tougher than the girl next to her just so she doesn't get her ass kicked.

Where I am timid and keep my thoughts to myself, she says what is on her mind—whenever it finds root there—and she doesn't hold anything back. When guys at clubs circle us while dancing—a way for them to show their appreciation in the hopes that one of us will give them our number— they begin to hoot and chant, "Go white girl! Go white girl!" when Diane dances, her body wildly and fiercely imitating dances she finds in music videos and other clubs she frequents in the Bronx and in Westchester. She gets in their faces, thrusting her chest out at them, and calls them out. I love this about her because I don't do this. I navigate the spaces around me trying to stay invisible, tucking myself into small corners that are safe, quiet, taking up as little-to-no space as possible. Diane walks and dances and moves through the spaces I share with her with confidence and derision.

I admire the voice she has that I lack, but where I am strong, she is weak. Love rules her, as do the boys she loves. When she falls for a guy, it is with such a heaviness that she disappears into them. I learn that when she meets a guy, I won't see her for a while, until she calls me up in the middle of the night to tell me he has cheated on her or dumped her or said something irredeemable to her and she needs permission to forgive him. I am not the forgiving type, so I tell her my thoughts, to dump him, to lose his number, to give her sex to him only if he's worth her time and sex. Usually, she ignores my advice, so I learn to hold back my tongue—keep my thoughts to myself. Her boyfriends usually hate me. I am the virgin friend, the feminist friend, the one who goes dancing three nights a week and moves from guy to guy without giving him what he deserves for his time and efforts. This is how they see sex. How they see girls.

Jacob hates me for sure. I give him a chance until he cheats on her and then I make it clear to her not to invite me to anything that involves him. But this is after Boo and I meet. Boo goes to school with Jacob, in Westchester, and it surprises me that they are friends. Boo is white, but very much like Diane. He is thuggish, big, and tough looking—more pudgy than solidly built. He has blonde hair and droopy blue eyes that look like slits opening up to look at you as if dragged out of sleep. He's a bit like a sloth, slow, chill, and laid back. I wonder if he's on drugs when I talk to him, because his phrases are sluggish, but I come to know that he is clean, smart, already conducting cancer research at NYU under the supervision of a scientist and professor who intends to publish it.

I think Boo should be going out with my smart and tough friend, but she is tied around the thin and lanky limbs of Jacob, and Boo kisses me across the booth at the diner we frequent in Astoria when we double-date. They both think he and I will get along and we do, but there is nothing between us except chemistry. Lots of it.

Jacob is vanilla white in contrast. He comes from a wealthy family, plays golf, and has not worked a day in his life. And when Diane tells him that I'm a virgin, he derides me at a lunch Diane has set up for us the first time we meet.

"How are you still a virgin?" he scoffs, eyeing me with suspicion.

"Not that it's any of your business," I retort, "but I choose to be."

"It's ridiculous! You're in your twenties. What, you want to stay a little girl forever?"

I arch my eyebrows at Diane, wondering if she will stand up for me, but she does not. She just sits there, looking at me, and I think I see a flicker of a smile slithering along her mouth. I realize then that even she thinks I am ridiculous for not having had sex yet. I mean, it's not like I haven't had opportunities. I have.

But why is it such a big deal if I don't want to have sex? That I like being a virgin? That I like governing my own choices and body? I will not be the girl who gives her sex up under pressure because those around me deem it ridiculous.

"My virginity is none of your business," I tell him, "and it's not up for discussion." Why does he care so much what I do or don't do with my body anyway? He acts as if I am a threat. Perhaps he thinks I will influence Diane into not having sex with him. Is that the fear? After this, a distance grows between me and Diane like a hearty, stubborn weed, and when she does make time to see me, Jacob does not join us.

But Boo and I continue to see each other. I invite him to Club Night at my school, and he and I dance, our hips grinding in unison to the bass of the DJ's selection, old John's eyes on me. He is a security guard still, long after he has graduated from our school. He is a father now. A husband. And it gives me a thrill to know that as I kiss Boo in a booth, Boo's mouth all over me, his arms keeping me in a tight embrace I can't get out of even if I wanted—and I don't—he only gets to look, and I revel in the pain this causes in him, watching his virgin give it to someone else. Of course, I am not giving it to Boo, either. I don't love him. Although he's an amazing kisser and he acts as if he really likes me, he's not loyal or honest—and I don't invest in guys like that.

On my birthday, he picks me up in his yellow jeep, the windows down, my hair assaulted by the wind we speed through on the highway leading to his rented basement room in a married friend's house. Boo babysits their kids when they go out on date nights, and for this night, my birthday night, they offer him their kitchen and oven so he can bake me a cake. It's a vanilla cake with chocolate frosting, "Happy Birthday, Boo" written in flowy pink letters across the top, a single candle set in the middle, its flame beckoning to be blown out.

This is the first time a boy has ever done anything for my birthday, let alone bake me a cake. Although my mother has baked me a few cakes during my years with her, she has never had parties for me. I have always wanted to know what it would be like to be the center of everyone's attention, to have an array of voices serenade me, their presence at my birthday party letting me know I am cared for, considered, loved. I have not known this, and even with all the boys I have dated and kissed and rolled around beds of sand with, I have not been with one who has made my birthday a special one.

He cooks me dinner, too—baked chicken with mashed potatoes and green beans on the side—but when the cake comes, I feel like an exuberant little girl given a drop of love for the first time in her life, looked upon by a set of deep blue eyes that take pride in surprising me, smiling in the happiness they have brought out in me. When he bids me to make a wish, I wish for this feeling to never end—this feeling of being loved and cherished—and I blow out the candle, inhaling the scents of burning wick and warm cake batter all at once.

When Boo kisses me, I am transported into another place and time, and my thoughts are transfixed on the mysterious ways my skin responds to him, his mouth, his fingers, the way our bodies slide from one wall onto the next adjoining one, ending up in a conjoined ball of legs and arms, connected hips and heads on the floor, on the bed, back against the wall, as if the force of our mouths meeting is a single firework set aflame in a small space, its energy propelling it from surface to surface in the room until it is contained and extinguished. His mouth on mine consumes me, and I love the sensation of being swallowed by him—not just by his mouth, but by his arms, his legs, his thighs—the way they wrap around me and make me disappear into the folds of all of him—finding myself inside his center, cradled there, consumed, overtaken, safe, loved.

I can probably let myself love him. I can, I think. Until we lie side by side on his bed, fully clothed, enfolded into the crook of his arm, and his phone rings. It's not what he says that makes the hairs at the nape of my neck rise, the lump in my throat dry up and tense. It's the tone in his voice as he says, "Hey. How are you? Yeah. Let me call you a bit later, okay, Boo?" It's soothing, low, husky, the way he speaks to me when I'm on the phone with him, when he calls me Boo, and this is when I know there is another girl on the line with him, and I make my body stiffen, constructing an impenetrable wall around the inner chambers of my heart yet again.

"I gotta go," I tell him, rising, withdrawing from his warmth, suddenly cast in a bubble of cold, detached air that chills me to the bone.

"What's the matter?" He reaches for me, but I evade his fingers.

"Nothing. It's late. I gotta get home or my mom will alert the police," I attempt a weak joke. I can't look at him. I can ask him who the girl was on the line, but at this point I don't care. The point is there is another girl. On the phone with him. In his life. And he acts like I'm the only one, baking for me, singing happy birthday to me, kissing me like I'm the only one.

Avoiding his gaze, I move to the door, ready to run out of his place and to the train station that will take me home.

"I'll drive you."

"Nah. I'm good."

"Can I see you this weekend?"

I stop my feet. I turn around. I am so tired all of a sudden. "This is the weekend I leave for Cancun," I tell him.

"Oh, yeah." He takes a few steps towards me, cups my chin, and tilts it up to force my eyes to meet his. I finally look at him, but I know what he sees. Ice. Disenchantment. None of the heat and desire he had found there before, when we had been kissing and rolling from surface to surface as if it meant something. Apparently, it all means nothing. It's just sex. Sex from me and sex from whichever girl he is talking to when he's not with me. Well, he can have her. I'm taking myself out of the equation.

"Call me when you get back. I'm serious about what I said before. I want to take you home to Virginia. My mom really wants to meet you."

"Yeah, sure." My voice is flat, and I'm sure he can hear it. "I'll call you." I already know I won't.

When I get home, I call Diane.

"Is he seeing other girls?" I ask her. She's my best friend, so I expect her to tell me the truth.

"Kath, I can't say anything. Jacob made me promise not to."

This confirms my suspicion. "Are you fucking kidding me?" I yell into the phone. "I'm your friend, Diane."

"I know, but he's my boyfriend. All I can say is that Michael really likes you. He's always talking about you to Jacob."

"How do you let me hang out with a guy and not warn me that he's seeing other girls?" I am shocked, and I realize at this point that my friendship with her is going to be different.

"Kath, I'm caught in the middle," Diane whines. "I can't betray Jacob's trust."

"You're not in the middle. You chose a side, and it's not mine. I gotta go. I'll talk to you later." With that, I hang up.

The next time I talk to Diane, it is a year later, when she calls me at two in the morning, crying. Jacob has cheated on her, and she doesn't know if she should take him back. I know better than to tell her what I really think. I let her talk, and I do what I am good at and my friends love about me: I listen. Without reproach. Without interruption. I take in the pain, the tears, the confusion. I am the sounding board for their indecisions, until they realize what they need to do. She goes back to him, and six months later, they break up for good. She calls me to hang out, and I go because she's still a friend, because I still care about her, because I know how devastating it is to be replaced and broken all at the same time. There is a yawning distance between us, and it has nothing to do with the physical spaces that keep us in opposite sides of the city.

I put Boo on hold while I travel to Cancun, and when I return from my trip, he calls. But I've already had a taste of the kind of relationship I want. The John kind of love. The Horacio kind of love. The double-dipping kind of love—or sex—he is offering is not what I am looking for.

He wants to take me to see his mother in Virginia. It will be an overnight trip, and I know what this means. Not happening. I tell him I'll call him later, but I never do. Eventually, he gives up. I have already moved on.

Janipp invites me out with Andrew from Cancun. She wants to go dancing in the city, so I say okay. When she and I step in line to enter the club, I come face to face with David, Andrew's buddy.

I smile weakly when he reaches over to hug me.

"You've been avoiding me," he says.

"No, I haven't." I feel my face grow red with shame and wish for the tan I had in Cancun to conceal it. He's called me a few times, but I keep letting the machine pick up.

"Yeah, you have. But it's okay. I get it. You were on vacation, now we're here. In real life."

"Yes" is all I can say. I like looking into his eyes, witnessing all the flavors of blue and green clashing and swirling into this unwavering gaze that locks on to my own. I am not drunk this time. I am sober. Awake. But I am shy with him, remembering the wanton feelings, the uninhibited touches we shared on the booze cruise. The way I ignored him the day they came to our hotel to surprise us and I only wanted more moments with Horacio.

"So, are you still with that kid from Mexico? The one from the hotel?"

We're in the club now, having showed our ID, and moving into the loud halls of the club, the sounds of the music splintering his words as they come at me, catching one word here, another word there, forcing me to bend my body towards his to hear him, enthralled by the whiff of his cologne that seems to pull me even closer.

"No. That was then. He's too far away for anything." I look away from him, wondering if he can see the loneliness that creeps and crawls beneath my skin like a disease finding comfort within the lines and sinews of my muscles.

"Do you want to go out with me sometime? After tonight? Just you and me?" Each phrase comes out one after the other, as if he can see the skittishness and discomfort I feel after the first question.

"Look," I begin. "I just broke up with someone, and I'm really tired of dating. I just want a break. I like you. I want to hang out, but I just can't handle anything else right now."

"Okay," he nods, grinning, his eyes flickering in the dim lights of the club, humoring me, it seems. "How about we start small. A dance?"

I sigh loudly and flash him a grin of my own. A genuine one. "Sounds good."

We move to the middle of the dance floor, where we find Andrew and Janipp, and the four of us dance until the club closes, and we part ways, Janipp and I heading to Queens, and the guys heading to the Bronx.

For the next few weeks, the four of us spend a lot of time together. David takes us to a Cuban restaurant in Queens; they pick us up in Andrew's car and we head to Jones Beach for the day, or Roosevelt Field Mall. At first, Dave is a gentleman. He doesn't even try to kiss me until the third time he sees me. The fourth time, I kiss him back. We are all in Andrew's parked car in Queens, after having gone to the movies. He kisses my ear during the film, my neck, runs his nails over my fingertips, tickling the palm of my hand and winking at me, the international signal for "I want to have sex with you."

Janipp and Andrew have already had sex. They're in love. Exclusive. Janipp wants to marry him, and he seems fixed on her. They went all the way to Mexico to meet and fall in love. Dave and I are not in love, and as much as I like him, I feel that he wants a replay of Cancun. But we are not in Cancun. We are home, and I am not under the influence of an illusory cloud of sex and alcohol. I am still a virgin looking for something more, something substantive. For a boy who sees me—not my sex.

Dave only sees sex. I know this about him when he kisses me, as if he wants to catch up to Andrew, to the lengths other girls have let him go with their bodies and wants. All the way.

I know this because when he and I are seated in the back seat of Andrew's car, with Janipp and Andrew making out in the front, Dave reaches for me and kisses me. His tongue is deep in my mouth and his hands rove over me with a hunger that surprises me. I don't believe his need is exclusively for me, for the love of me, the touch of me—his hunger is blind and overwhelming and has nothing to do with me. I am just there. I have all the parts his hunger seeks. I have the mouth, the breasts, the thighs, and all the stuff in between needed to feed him. I try to slow down his kiss, placing my hand against his chest to signal he stop. He does. He breathes into my hair, and then takes my hand and places it on his crotch, throbbing beneath the fabric of his shorts and pushing against my fingers. I take my hand back as if it has touched fire.

"Why are you so afraid of it? I can't tell you how good it feels when you touch me. You excite me." He whispers this so our friends don't hear him.

"I'm not afraid of your penis," I tell him with an attitude. "I'm just afraid of dicks who force me to do things I don't want to do." I hear Janipp laugh from the front and Andrew shush her. They turn on the radio to drown out the argument they believe my words will ensure.

"Look, I'm tired of going home with blue balls," he tells me, and I have to think for a bit as to what this means—blue balls. When I get it, I turn a look of disgust in his direction.

"It's not my job to fix this problem of yours." I move to the opposite side of the car and clench my teeth together.

"Well, you gave them to me. It's only right."

I look at him and he winks at me. I'm not sure if he is joking or if this is what he really thinks. "Are you kidding me right now?"

"Look, Kathy. I like you. A lot. I just want to take our relationship a bit farther. We can't just kiss like teenagers all the time. That's great, but I want more than that."

"Well, kissing is as far as I am willing to go, so you should find yourself someone else for the more that you want." I look out the window, frustration pressing against my temples.

"So that's it?"

"Yes."

"Fine."

There is an awkward silence from the front of the car, and after a few seconds, Andrew starts the engine. He lets me out first, and I run out of the car without saying a word to anyone.

Dave calls a few times after that, but I don't pick up, listening to his voice on my machine only after he hangs up.

I see him six months later at a party he has in his home. He has invited Andrew and Janipp, and she brings me along, saying he has asked for me. But I drink a lot, out of boredom and loneliness, and he finds me sitting alone in his living room, most of his party guests outside by the pool, drinking, dancing, breaking through the surface of the crisp blue water fully clothed, laughter and alcohol dancing wildly inside them.

I feel alone. I have not dated since Dave, and I swim in angry waters of self-loathing, wondering what it is about me boys can't see long enough to stay. If they stayed, if they waited patiently until I was ready, until I felt seen and loved, sex would come easy for me. But these boys are impatient. Horny, and when one girl says no, they move on to the next. We girls are expendable. What one girl doesn't give, another one will.

Dave sits next to me, the movement of his body making me shift in my own seat of depression. He places his arm around my shoulders, and I want to cry into his. They are so perfect and soft and warm, and I want to find my home in them. Even if it's just for this one night. He traces a finger along my cheek, tilts my face up to his, and then slides his tongue over my lips and into my mouth for a drink. I taste the Coke and gin that he has been drinking all night, watching me over his glass, and I wonder what he tastes in mine. Probably the beer I have been consuming red cup after red cup since the minute I walked through the door of his home, bombarded by memories of Cancun and Dave and how it felt to be wanted by someone.

When he places his hands under my shirt, moves his fingers up to my bra and unhooks it, I let him. My arms are too tired to stop him. I'm too tired of stopping him and all the boys I have stopped so far. And I want this. I want his touch, his hands cupping my breasts and his fingers squeezing my nipples. I arch my back, pressing more of me into him, submitting to him, his hands, his mouth, growing hungrier by the second. He doesn't care that I am drunk. And I am too numb to care. I will care tomorrow. Tonight, this feels good. Too good to stop.

He pulls away from me, grabs my hand and pulls me off the couch, leading me to the laundry room. Closing the door, he tries to pull my shirt off, but I shake my head. I feel him tense, so I reach up and kiss him, my hand finding its way to the bulge I had rejected months earlier, cupping it in my own hands, rubbing it, and reveling in the sigh that he releases in my own mouth. My fingers please him, and I like being the source of his pleasure. It feels good to please someone else—not just to feel pleasure but to give it. But I also feel the resistance rise from my belly into my throat, like a scream that wants to be given a voice. I subdue her. Quiet her.

I want this, I tell her. *Shut the fuck up.*

You're drunk, she tells me. *You'll hate yourself tomorrow.* She knows me.

That's tomorrow. Let me have this. I just want to feel good. I want to feel something.

It won't feel good tomorrow, she reminds me, and I know this to be true. But I am drunk, reeling in liquor and how good it feels to have someone's hands hot and desirous on my skin, to hold his desire for me in my hands and feel the power that comes with making his own pleasure rise and throb, like holding his heart in the palm of my hands, feeling its pulse growing strong and wild because of me. Little old me. Little plain me. Little virgin me.

And although this power feels good for the moment—this moment in which I am drunk and not in my full senses—I know, deep down, that this is not the kind of power I want to yield over boys. I don't want them to want sex from me. I want them to love me. Just one of them. And sex and love, when they don't come together, joined at the ribcage, is not what I want. But at this moment, I let Dave's hands and mouth tamp down my needs as if they are burdensome children pulling at our ankles for attention.

Dave pushes me against the surface of the door, pins my hands above my head, kisses me hard and good, and grinds his erection against my own burning thighs. I grind back and smile when he groans.

He brings one of my hands down from above my head and

places it on his crotch. I imagine it's because he wants me to feel how much he wants me. But I could be any girl, I remind myself, so it's not a want of me, but a want of any girl's hands cupping his desire. Silencing the warning voice seething in my head, I do what he wants me to do with my hand, willing my fingers to unzip his tan shorts and pull out the soft, hard attachment that broke us up in the first place. I caress it and wrap my fingers tightly around its width, wanting to feel its fullness pulsating against the palm of my hand, this thing that rules boys' thoughts and actions, deciding for them which girl to date, which girl to screw, which girl to love, and which girl to abandon when she does not submit to its demands. Its ultimatums.

This is my first time doing this. Dave is the first boy I have done this to, and it surprises me that I know what to do when my only knowledge of it has come from my Harlequin romances. My hand naturally, longingly pulls on it, squeezes it, releases it, and then pulls it again, encasing it in the warm and sweaty grip of my hand, a mock grasp of the womb it really wants to be enfolded in. I like the way his breathing staggers and falls into mine, the way he whispers my name against my neck, and my hand quickens and tightens. Is this what they really want? Is this what I have to do to keep them, to find love in them? Is what I want, what I need of no importance?

"Kathy," his voice is husky, full, wonderful to hear because it tells me that I have pleased him, and it makes my pulse flutter in the pit of my belly. "If you don't want to go further, then you have to stop."

He pulls me up, cups my face with his hands, and kisses me again. "It's okay if you want to stop. I want you, but if you're not ready . . ." He lets the rest of his message trail off.

"I'm not ready," I murmur and look away from him with shame. I can't do more. I know it, drunk or otherwise. There is a part of me that wants to give in, to want more, but not with Dave. He's not the one—even if he does kiss me so well and his touches turn me into a simpering wanton every time. He's not the boy I want to have sex with. Now or ever. And having sex with him would be a waste because I know he hasn't been pining over me. I know he's had girls before me, during me, and after me. I know because Janipp tells me everything.

"He is a player. There is a different strand of hair on his pillow for every day of the week," she warns me the night at the party when she finds me watching him over my third beer.

"She loves this analogy," nudges Andrew, and laughs at her creativity with words. Andrew nods his head at me in agreement. "Watch yourself with him." And this comes from his best friend.

But I ignore all this when the chemistry is exhumed between us at his first touch, his first kiss, the tenderness he shows me even after I have rebuked him.

We make ourselves presentable by picking up shorts and hooking bras and straightening the wrinkles in our shirts and the mussiness of our hair, and, holding hands, we go back out to the party, wild and loud, by the poolside. When it's time to leave, Dave walks me to Andrew's car, opens the back door for me, and kisses me tenderly, his wispy voice promising to call me.

"I want to see you again, Kathy."

"Okay," I say under the weight of his mouth on mine and get in the back seat. Once on the road, the drive from the Bronx to Queens seems never ending and a bile rises from deep in my throat. I am sober now, awake, shame trailing over my flesh, every part of my skin still burning from the memory of his fingers, his lips, his tongue, like a slithering snake winding around me, squeezing, pushing all the air out of my lungs by force. Andrew has to pull over, and I rush out of it, fall on my knees, and throw up all the liquor, all the sexual feelings unloosened and given expression, all over the patchy green weeds outlining the highway we need to get back on to go home.

But the memories stay. They stain everything. I avoid mirrors so as not to locate the whore in my features and bathe twice a day in hopes that with each scrub of soap and water, my wantonness will be gutted from my pores, bleed into the soapy water, and trail into the pipes, lost forever, erasing the shame sticking to me like semen, a stubborn and unyielding reminder that once you lose a part of you, once you give it away like the whore your mother knows you are, there is no way to get it back.

When Dave calls, I ignore him, letting him go to my machine. I burrow deeper into my blankets, twisting the memory of him, of me, of us, drunk and stupid and sexy, between my legs and sheets in an attempt to strangle them all to death.

A VIRGIN'S WRATH

Anger becomes my new friend, my shield, and I wield her power with protective fervor. I decide I will not let my feelings for a boy —any boy—turn me into the girl I don't want to be. I disentangle my roots from people who will take me in that direction— like Janipp. But she is so involved with Andrew she doesn't notice my disappearance. She has also disappeared, into Andrew, and I no longer see her at VIM.

I work at the jean store without her. I still have my job at the library, but the jean store pays more, an actual minimum wage, and I can still afford to pay for my tuition and have enough left over to give my mother rent money. I throw myself into school and work. I still date, but I make sure I only take what I need and I give only what I want to give. I am selfish, as these boys are, but I am selfish for the sake of self-preservation. No one cares for me as I do. No one will endeavor to fight for me with the intensity and love that I will fight for myself.

I know this because not even my mother fights for me. Why should the boys I meet at a club or in one of my classes or in the student union at my college? They take and take, not caring about the mess they leave behind when they move on to the next girl they want to take. I don't want to be on this path—boys taking and taking from me until there is nothing of me left—the real me—the one I respect and care for in a way that no one will care for no matter how sweetly they croon their love for me.

And they do. Croon their love. Whisper it in my ear, their fingers tangled in my hair, tugging at it as if to entice me, prove to me their love. But I see what they want. Sex. And more sex. Not me. How could they love me? They've gone on three, maybe four dates with me. Love doesn't happen in an instant. Love happens over time, when two people know each other, every single spark and flaw that exists, and then stay—despite the flaws, the angers, the disappointments that cling to us like wet silk, soft and sheer and twisted around our necks with the ease of a stranglehold. When you see it all and stay, that is love. And this doesn't happen after one date or one month—the longest I stay in a relationship with a boy for the next three years. John, the first one, has been my longest relationship at three months.

I meet yet another John in one of my classes. He's Greek, and he wants to take me dancing one night after work. It's Saturday and I have the evening shift at the jean store. I won't have time to change between work and my date, so I go to work dressed up. I wear a red buttoned-down shirt with frilly sleeves that slip off at the elbows, a tight black mini-skirt, and high heels. When my supervisor sees me, she arches her eyebrow and tells me to man the entrance of the store. This job is intended for a guard, but we don't have one tonight.

It doesn't take long for me to realize that she is using me for bait, and I don't know how to feel—angry, disappointed, or flattered. I feel flattered until I am bombarded with pairs of eyes belonging to men that clash with mine. I don't meet these gazes, flushing. I then get angry because I feel exposed, standing by the entrance to the store, the mall full of male gazes travelling up and down my body as if they have a right to—as if I want them to see me, to experience me in this way.

In the end I am disappointed with my supervisor, a young woman in her thirties who I have looked up to for her ability to manage a store all by herself, commanding both respect and fear from her employees. When she promotes me to lead cashier, I love her even more, thinking she has seen the hard and responsible worker that I am. It is a position only the most trustworthy girls are promoted to, especially since we have to work with money, count it each evening to make sure none of it is missing, mark it in the books, and ensure it is locked away in the safe before closing. But on this evening, she forfeits any respect I have for her. She is like a man, as placing a younger girl by the door to entice onlookers and prospective male shoppers with her sex appeal is something I would have only expected another man to do—not a woman. I expect women to protect young girls since they have already gone through the sexist gauntlet of entitled eyes grazing against skin and curves without permission, without consent, as if we are pieces of meat to be tossed into the hungry mouths of men.

The eyes, hisses, and whistles don't make me feel proud, sexy. They have the opposite effect. My shoulders droop with an ache, my chest caves into itself, and my head hangs with shame. This is worse than increasing my sexual experience by touching Dave, and the residual echo of his mouth on my skin clashes with the unknown male glances stripping me that I want to block from penetrating my body.

At this point, three boys pass me as they enter the store. They all make the effort to press their eyes over my body so that I can feel the weight of them, these eyes that take and take against my will.

"You have a great future behind you," one of them grins at me and the rest of the boys start laughing. Is this funny? I'm supposed to make a future from my ass?

"Assholes," I hiss back, only evoking more laughter from them. They have the power—the power to look me over, to assess my potential desirability, to consume me with just their eyes, and let me know that I am nothing more than an object. A thing. Not Kathy. Not a virgin. Not a person of significance with feelings and interests and needs. Just a body of parts that have the potential to please them, either through a gaze or more, while the rest of me, the unwanted parts—the undesirable parts, like the mind, the self, the person—are all muted and blotted out because they are of no consequence to their needs. Who teaches boys this? That girls are consumable objects, things, immutable parts for the taking?

An image, tattered and browned by time, crawls to my vision. It is the memory of a woman with dark, tangled hair, sitting on a park bench, her skirt hiked up mid-thigh, revealing the muscled contours of her legs, letting men know she can be bought for a few minutes to an hour, while I play a few feet away in the sandbox of the children's park. I watch her lead men behind trees, sometimes to nearby hotels, her eyes leaving theirs for the length of time it takes to warn me to stay in place until she returns. It feels like forever to a little girl my age, playing alone, wondering if she will ever come back. But she does, sitting on the bench, winking at me as she counts her money. Her name is Athanasia, and she is the mother whose body spit me out into a life I try with a vengeance to avoid. And yet here I am, having my own body, which I protect with stubborness, being exploited and yawned open by strange men who would liken me to someone like her—as if we were all the same, here for one purpose. Sex.

I storm to the back of the store where my manager, Christina, is counting cash, her pink manicured nails flashing quickly through the air.

"Christina," I begin, blowing the wisps of my bangs off my forehead. "I am not comfortable standing out there. I feel completely exposed. Can I do something else? Please?" The last part almost comes out in tears, and I realize I have been trying to hold them back. It is humiliating standing there, in my club night outfit, used for my sex to bring in clients. That's what prostitutes do. What my birth mother did. And it is the opposite of how I want to live my life. I am not that mother.

She tells me to go in the stockroom, where I can unpack clothes from boxes and use the price gun to tag each item with price stickers. I smile at her, and when I enter the back room, I am glad for the dark space absent of men, their low whistles and penetrating stares.

Perhaps it's the outfit. Maybe it's the skirt that makes them all want to treat me like a whore, the way the spandex fabric hugs and clings to my butt and thighs, revealing my lean legs. Maybe it's the heels, the way they make me look taller, as if I'm standing on my toes, outlining the muscular contours of my calves and thighs. Maybe it's the red shirt. It's not revealing, but it is red, the color of sex and desire.

"If you dress like that, people will treat you like it," I recall my mother's voice saying to me only a few hours earlier when she steals a glance at my appearance before I leave.

"Dress like what?" I ask her, already knowing the answer to her warning.

"You know. Like a whore." It's been a while since she's called me that, but it's not a surprise to me when I feel the sting of her intended insult.

She is right. It's my fault. Everyone has treated me like a whore in this outfit, even my female supervisor, so maybe there's truth in her statement. The way I dress lets people know how to treat me. And I don't want anyone to treat me like this anymore. I don't like all these eyes on me. I want to collect all of their eyeballs, like marbles, seal them in a jar, and stare back at them. See how they like it. I want to lash out, blind them, yank them out of the hungry sockets they belong to, rip their grins off their faces, tear into their heads and take back the image of me they have taken without my consent, devouring it, sullying it with their gross and vile fantasies—fantasies I have no control over and which only serve to defile me, the virgin, a girl they don't know but who they see as a whore. Simply because she's a girl.

When John meets me outside at the end of my shift, I am feeling vulnerable in my outfit. Will he take me for a whore also? So far, he is a gentleman. He offers to buy me a drink, but I only drink with my friends now—never with boys. I ask for a bottle of water, and when we're ready we make our way to the center of the floor to dance. Moving in unison with him, I take in his black wavy hair, his brown eyes, and the twin dimples resting on either side of his cheeks, widening whenever he smiles. There's no chemistry between us, and I don't have a desire to kiss him. When he does kiss me, it's okay. There is nothing behind it to make me lean into him for more.

I take a sip of my water. Maybe it's okay to like someone who doesn't make you feel reckless and hot inside. So far, all the boys who have made me feel this way—out of control with desire—have wanted more from me than I can give them. Maybe John won't. He's a Greek boy. Maybe his family has taught him to respect girls, to wait and get to know them before he tries to cop a feel of the buds bursting beneath their tank tops. Perhaps I have been dating the wrong guys this whole time. Maybe.

I have fun with John. He is funny and cute, and he keeps his hands to himself. We dance until midnight, and then he drives me home. With his car still running, he bends towards me and kisses me goodnight. There is nothing else. Just a kiss. A soft, easy kind of kiss that promises to come back for me.

The next morning, John calls me to tell me he had a good time and asks if I want to do it again.

"Sure," I say.

"*Putana!*" I hear a woman's voice in the background, spitting the term through the line as if it can grab me by the throat and squeeze. "What kind of girl keeps boys out so late at night?"

"What?" I half laugh with disbelief on my side of the phone.

"I'm sorry," he says to me. "Mama, *stamata,*" he whispers thickly to the woman I take as his mother, telling her to stop in our mutual Greek tongue.

"Your mother just called me a *putana?*" I ask him for confirmation.

"Yeah, I'm so sorry. She's just pissed that we stayed out late."

"So, are you a whore, too, for coming home late, or is it just me?" I can't hide the snark in my tone, but mostly, I'm more irritated with the fact that he tries to shush her, unsuccessfully, but he doesn't stand up for me. He doesn't tell her that I am not a whore. That I'm a good girl.

"Just let me call you later. Okay?" He asks.

"Sure," I tell him but already know I won't be picking up the phone when he does call. I won't date a guy who doesn't stand up for me, even to his mother. And I don't need another Greek mother calling me a *putana* when she doesn't know me for shit. One is enough.

When the phone rings, I stare at it, but I don't move to get it. My eyes instead note the outfit I wore at the club with John and at my job, my boss using me to entice men into the store, the memory of the birth mother I try to forget. I pick up the skirt and top and toss them into the trash. No more miniskirts for me. No more red colors for me. No more heels. Ever. Jeans, T-shirts, flannel shirts tied at the waist, and combat boots beckon me like a beacon of light, pulling me in to safety from the treacherous waters of male desire and objectification threatening to scrape me against the rock's jagged edges until I am knocked unconscious and drown—until I am nothing more than a ghost-impression of myself.

HOW TO WHORIFY A VIRGIN

I throw myself into work, taking a break from guys for a while. My heart fractures a little each time I meet one and then break up with one, all because they want more than I can give. They seem to take a piece of me with them when they walk away, as unsatisfied as I am, but for different reasons. They want sex. I want love. I won't have one without the other. And in the end, I am left all alone with only my principles to hold me when I weep.

"So why are you still a virgin?" Craig, a friend at school from our Jewish Club asks, looking at me with a thoughtful gaze one day as we sit in the Jewish Club room at the student union of our school. He's not Jewish either, with his solid six-foot-three build, blonde hair, and blue eyes, finding solace in the people and club of Jewish kids who accept all kind of strays like us.

I shrug my shoulders. "I just haven't found anyone I want to have sex with," I tell him with a frankness I have learned to adopt whenever anyone discovers I am a virgin. It has traveled to ears far and wide along our campus, and I am like a rare bird they look at from a distance. I am a twenty-something virgin and it's unfathomable. There must be something wrong with me—something they cannot see, so they dig into me with piercing eyes and questions, probing through words and experiences I share with them, examining every phrase with a microscope to uncover the reasons for this thing I am, this oddity that continues to exist despite the world's perversions, its insistence to slough off innocence with the ferocity of a hard scrubbing brush intended to remove the layers of dead, unwanted skin.

My sex is not something I want to scrape off me or exfoliate, as if it's dead, unwanted scraps of skin still holding on to me. I want it. I want it the way I want love to come and surrender his secrets to me, enfolding me into silk sheets of security and solace, the way I want to find a boy who loves me—me, not my sex. Sex alone is not what I want, no matter how much pressure I come across from both the boys I date and the girls who look at me as if I'm some silly Peter Pan girl who doesn't want to grow up even as my body matures and desires. This is what I want, and I don't care about the looks they give me or the pieces of my heart they snip off each time I say no and they walk away.

I go to the library in the mornings and work my four-hour shifts, finding corners to read from a collection of books I have hidden in the stacks. When my shifts coincide with Lina's, a beautiful, small Chinese girl I befriend, we talk about her latest exploits with her boyfriend Gary, and she invites me to a party her sorority is giving in Flushing. She goes to St. John's University, and sometimes, I cut my own classes and sit in on hers, just to hang out, just to get away from campus and people and classes that hold no more secrets or excitement for me. We dance together, drink together, and attend parties at St. John's that serve as a distraction from the sadness that has begun to creep beneath my skin, finding root in my bones, scraping against the raw skin of my bruised hopes and expectations.

In the evenings, I go to the jean store at the mall with half a heart pumping air into me. One night during the Christmas rush, I work as a cashier, taking care of two teen-aged girls. The line is long behind them, I am one of three cashiers, and the assistant manager is on the floor eyeing us, making sure we move quickly. The line tapers off. When I tell the girls how much they owe, they giggle, throw a smirk in my direction, and tell me, "We don't want it anymore. Thanks."

I heave a long, frustrated sigh. I need a void and only the assistant manager can give it to me since she has the key to the register.

My eyes cast out past the crowd to find her. Tall, thick, a tight ponytail set against her scalp pulling back her black hair, Renee arches her eyebrows at me.

"I knew that was going to happen," she tells me over the bobbing heads of customers, the line growing longer since this void is holding me up.

"Can I get a void then?" I can't conceal the exasperation budding in my voice.

She stands in her spot, continues to stare at me, and shakes her head instead. "I knew it," she repeats. "You didn't see it coming?"

"Can I get a fucking void then?" Each word shoots out of me like a thorn aimed for blood. I can't understand why she still stands there when she could just come and give me a void so I can move to the next customer.

Without a word, she comes behind the counter, places her key in my register, turns it, and punches a few keys to give me the void. We both go on as if nothing happened until the end of my shift when she tells me to go home and not come back.

This is the first time I have been fired. I am humiliated. I storm out of the store, walk home, crawl into my bed, and cry.

It's not just the shame that keeps me in bed for the next four days. It's the feeling of helplessness that comes with needing a job. My library job will not pay for my tuition alone, and I don't know how to continue with school if I can't pay for it. I consider asking my mother for help, but I push away the thought. Her help comes with conditions, being home by eight, not dating, not going to clubs or dancing. Just school. Just work. Just home with her. I will die—inside—if I can only be with the woman whose approval comes with complete obedience and self-erasure. I won't condemn myself to invisibility, to conformity—to a woman who lives with me like a stranger, prying me open with eyes that profess to know me and only see the worst in me.

At the end of four days, my mother has had enough of my sulking and comes into my room with a newspaper clipping from the help-wanted ads.

"This looks like a good job for you." She places the paper on my pillow, stained with the grease from my unwashed hair. "Get up. Take a shower. Eat something. Then call them."

I look at the position. It's a job at a television and rental company in Woodside. "Mom, this is not for me. They want someone to work in hospitals and rent the equipment to patients. I can do that, but it also says I have to connect the television sets and be able to fix them. I know nothing about that. It's a waste. . . . Thanks, though." I say this as an afterthought, pulling the covers over my head again, wishing life would stop at this point. Just let me press into my depression as if it is a pillow held tightly over my mouth and nose until my breaths no longer come rushing out of me.

"You never know," she continues as she makes her way to the door of my room, a room full of clothes tossed on the floor, a pile of unwashed plates with crusted food laying on my furniture, dust collected in layers on top of my things: picture frames, jewelry boxes, a pile of Harlequin romance books with lovers in mid-kiss silhouetted on the front covers I have yet to read but have borrowed from the library.

When I don't seem persuaded by her advice, she continues. "You go in for the interview anyway, even if you don't have the qualifications for this position, and who knows? Maybe they'll have something else for you. It's better than what you're doing right now. You're not going to get a job lying in bed." I hear her slippers scrape the floor as she exits, goes down the hall, and enters her own room, closing the door behind her.

This is who we are. Who we have become. I live in my room. She lives in hers. We don't eat together anymore, and when she cooks, it's only for her. I fend for myself. When I am really, really hungry, I will eat something from her refrigerator, but mostly, I try not to. I live on French fries from McDonald's or fruit I can buy from the Asian markets lining Queens Boulevard, the displays sporting large juicy peaches in the summer and green apples all year round. It's not that she forbids me from eating her food—hers because she has purchased it—it's more that I don't want to take things from her—including food. If I want my independence from her, then I have to go all the way. And yes, I know that all the way means moving out, but I can't afford to move out. If I do, then I will have to quit school and find a full-time job. I don't want to quit school or postpone it. I must get my education. It will ensure not only my independence from her but also that I do not end up the whore she expects me to be. I will get my education, then look for a decent job, save up, and move out. In that order. I just have to be patient. I must subdue the hungers railing against my ribcage not just for food but for love, for self-reliance, for having the only voice to define me based on terms that speak the truth of me: kind, good, honorable.

I go back into the precarious folds of life outside of my room and from beneath the sweaty sheets cocooning me. I make the call and land an interview. Dressed in black pants and a nice white buttoned-down shirt, I sit before my interviewer, Heidi Greenberg, the one who hires everyone for this small but thriving company. She asks me a few questions about my previous experience with selling, and after a while, she smiles at me and places her folder with my application on the table beside her.

"Listen," she begins. "I like you and think you will be a great fit for our company, but you're too small for this kind of job. I usually give it to guys because sometimes you have to pull down television sets from the wall, and I don't think you can do that."

The smile fades from my face, and I know she can read the disappointment as if I have opened the pages of my book for her to read the sad and woeful words breathing there, quietly abiding in tremulous but permanent ink.

"I'm going to remember you, though, and if I have anything else—something you're more suited for—I will recommend you and call you myself. Okay?"

"Yes," I nod and smile back at her even though I know the lines of my mouth rise weakly, pressured to lift and expand by her reassurance. "Thank you for your help," I offer along with my handshake, which I keep firm and solid in her warm clasp.

A week passes and school begins, but I keep looking for work to no avail. My tuition is due, and I enter a payment plan with the bursar's office to pay for it in five installments. This gives me a bit more time to find a job.

And then I get a call. But not from Heidi. The voice on the other side of the line belongs to a manager in the same company, Steve, and he asks me when I can begin work.

"Today," the words rush out.

He laughs. "How about tomorrow?" He gives me details about the position and a bunch of other words to go with them, but I don't hear any of it. I just know I begin tomorrow and that it pays more than the library and more than my last job at the jean store.

When I arrive the next morning, Steve looks me up and down from his side of the desk.

"Are you doing this on purpose?" His look is cold, and I feel my skin burn under the brown flecks of derision staring out at me from behind his glasses.

"What?" I stutter.

"Are you trying to prove something?" He brushes his fingers through his wavy black hair and rises from his seat to lead me to the conference room.

"I don't know what you mean," I reply, waving my hands up at my sides to show my confusion.

"I told you on the phone to wear a skirt. You're wearing pants. All women must wear skirts here. I told you this specifically on the phone."

I swallow the information with unsavory gulps, as if the words are chunks of liver being forced down my throat, reminding me of the time my mother sat opposite me at the dinner table until I tasted it and when I did, I had to spit it out and wipe the taste off my tongue with a slew of napkins.

"Honestly, Steve, I didn't hear you. I was so excited you called me in for the job, that I didn't hear a word you said yesterday."

He gives me a look as if he's not sure whether to believe me or not.

"I promise you. I would never do something like this on purpose. It's not me." My words are earnest, and I pray he can see the obedient girl that abides behind them.

"Well, do you have a problem wearing skirts to work? The owner of this company is Jewish, and he insists that all women wear skirts, so if it's a problem, just let me know."

"Not at all," I lie. In my head, I'm trying to think of which skirts I still own that I can wear to work. I got rid of most of them after my supervisor at the jean store used me as sex-bait for male customers. I haven't worn a skirt since.

"Alright then," he continues. "Let's go and get you trained. I'll introduce you to the rest of the girls in the counting room."

He takes me into a closed room that has one door and one square frame of the wall that opens to his side of the desk. We answer to him, to Steve, and our job entails counting the money that comes to the office from the hospitals. It's all cash, and we take bags of money from the safe, count it on the counting machines, write down the money on a sheet, tally it at the end of the day, and make sure it all balances. We pack the money up for the bank and put it back in the safe. I work with three other girls, and once I get the hang of the job and the calculator, my fingers punching down the buttons with speed and out of memory, we all race to see who will count the most money the fastest. Of course, who counts the most has a lot to do with who gets the cash from the biggest hospitals. NYU and Winthrop are hospitals that have the most money, so then we rush to work each morning to have first dibs on the big money bags, and the race begins.

I like my new job. The girls are all in college and fun to talk to, but we don't hang out after work or outside of work at all. We only see each other at work, and this suits me. I sit on my butt for hours, counting money, sometimes talking, sometimes not talking at all, and my only responsibility is to count and tally and balance. I even get to work overtime, getting paid time and a half, and the money comes to me in a small envelope with my name on it, in cash. I learn to hide in this job. I work on the weekends, all by myself, and Steve learns to count me in on holidays like Christmas Day, New Year's Day, Thanksgiving Day, and Fourth of July. Whenever everyone else opts to spend these precious days with family, I am at work, making money, avoiding the home that feels like I'm being buried alive, the mother to whom I can't speak, my fingers no longer itching to touch her, the feel of her having faded from memory the way the stars hide behind hazy layers of cloudy skies.

My jobs, my school, they all serve as escape from pangs of depression striking like a hammer against my head, pulling me under, my breath catching and breaking, longing for the reprieve that doesn't come unless I am away from her, away from her piercing eyes and words that make me feel like nothing.

I love my job because it keeps me from her, but I hate wearing skirts when I can wear jeans or even black dressy pants. There is a new hire, a girl who comes in and sits beside me so I can train her, but she quits after three days, using the words "bull shit" to show her disdain for the rules of this sexist company.

"You should quit, too," she tells me, packing her stuff and getting up from the cubicle next to me to leave. "You don't need this kind of job." But I cannot leave. I need the money. I have to pay for school. I am not her. I envy her because I am not like her.

I wish I was strong like her—confident enough to leave a job I don't like and confident enough to know that I can find another job. But I don't want to end up in bed again, crying again, helpless again, my mother being the only one to come to my rescue, feelings of indebtedness circling around us like vultures diving for scraps on carcass remains.

I don't quit. I wear skirts, as I am expected to, and feel male eyes burn through the fabric of them, trying to scrape through the seams to discover what is hidden behind the soft cotton fabric of my clothes. One day, a Saturday, I am in front of Steve's desk and reach into the frame of the window looking into our counting room, just to pull an envelope out of that room into this one, the one where all the managers—all men except for one woman—work behind their desks. A college kid who drives the vans, picking up the bags of money from the hospitals and bringing them to the office for us girls to count, stands behind me. He passes me, reaches his hand out, and smacks me hard on my ass. My face is beet red, and I feel blood rushing through me like a raging fire.

"Fucking asshole," I yell at him, looking around to see if anyone else has noticed what he has done. Because it's a Saturday, around six thirty, it is slow and quiet, with no one else in the room.

"I'm sorry," the blonde, blue-eyed boy chuckles. "I just couldn't help myself. It was right there, asking for it."

"You're a fucking pig," I sputter after him as he jogs to the back of the building where the drivers live and eat and breathe.

I wonder what the girl who quit would have done. I don't do anything other than yell at him. I tell the other girls when I see them on Monday, and they look at me sympathetically, but there's nothing they can do either. I need my job, so I don't want to cause any waves to go against me—I flow with the current, protecting myself when I need to. I find longer skirts to wear, ones that don't make my butt look tight and smackable. Skirts that hide the secret curves of my body, a body that wants to breathe and move without being noticed, ingested by gluttonous eyes and hands that mark it as something public and open for business.

A major part of my job I don't like is taking lunch orders. Only the girls do this, the money counters. We ask the managers, all men except for Beth, the only middle-aged female manager at the company, which menu they want—Italian, Chinese, Greek, Mexican—and then we take orders from all of them and call it in. When the food comes, we are also required to serve them their lunch. I don't like serving people. If I did, I would get a job as a food server. None of us likes this job, but we do it because it's expected of us. We're lowly, and we're girls.

"I want to eat some Greek today," one of the managers says to me, winking. He says this to me every time it's my turn to take lunch orders. I learn to roll my eyes the way the older girls at the company roll their eyes when it's their turn and he says he wants to eat Mexican today or Italian. We are used to it. We roll our eyes and change the conversation.

"Everyone wants Italian today," I tell him. "What would you like from the menu?"

Steve, because he deals with us directly is more careful about his actions. He jokes, he teases, but without using sexual innuendo. Until he does.

After being with the company for a year and watching girls come and go, I ask him for a letter of reference. It is my last year at Queens College for my undergraduate degree, and I want to apply for a volunteer job on campus, being a Big Buddy for homeless kids in the area. It's voluntary, but we get credit and a grade for it, and I need to raise my GPA from the semester I screwed up my grades when John—the first one—broke up with me. I wanted to apply to graduate school, pursuing a degree in English and secondary education, and this program is housed by the education department at Queens College. It serves many of my needs as I move forward with my education towards a career in teaching high school English, and I need a letter of recommendation just to get an interview.

Steve writes one for me while we are at work. He calls me to his desk and hands it to me, giggling like a child as I read it silently in front of him. It begins this way:

To whom it may concern:

*I highly recommend Kathy for the voluntary position as a
Big Buddy for homeless kids. I wish she were my Big
Buddy. She is sexy and hot and will make a fine candidate.*

The letter goes on for a full page focusing on my physical attributes and potential as a sex buddy. I read each word in a blur, and when I get to his signature, I raise my eyes to his. They flicker and twinkle with humor, as if he has done the funniest thing in the world, but all I feel is exposed, like a gutted fish, sliced in half, bleeding on his shoes. He is in his forties, a white generic male with a growing pouch in his mid-section. My eyes fall to the picture frame on his desk. In the family portrait, he stands beside his small brown-haired wife and their two sons, around ten and twelve years of age.

The paper shakes in my fingers, and I stand before him

wordlessly. What exactly am I supposed to say to this? And to whom do I say it? I really like him, so it annoys me that he is showing me another side to him that I find repulsive. A bubble of distrust begins to grow inside me, and I realize I cannot trust him. My knees are weak beneath the weight of the list of men I don't trust, men and boys who look at me and see sex and a thing they can sexualize—not a young girl in her early twenties trying to find her footing in this place that disgusts her more and more each day she wakes into it.

I feel the way I did when I was eleven and my trusted violin teacher asked me to sit on his lap, placing his shaky and freckled hands under my shirt to feel the bare skin hidden by my T-shirt. I sat there, biting my lip, trying to muster the courage to punch him, to get off his lap, to say the words that would remind him how wrong this was, but I sat there quietly, holding my breath, so afraid to speak or move, praying his hands did not sneak to the front of my still-flat chest. But his hands remained on the back, drawing circles along the flesh I hid even then, my spine curving into itself in an attempt to disappear.

When he was done with me, he handed me twenty dollars, the cost of my lesson. I returned one more time, hoping it was a one-time thing, but he did it again. I sat on his bony, aged legs and held my breath until he was done. He paid me again, and when I got home, I tore the money into so many pieces no one could make out it had ever been cash. I made my mother change music schools, and I never saw him again, but he returns to me every time a man turns me into a whore, a slut, a *putana* against my will, against my own desires. Like Steve just did. Another man I trust. My boss. A family man who works as closely as he does with so many young girls my age, training us, teaching us how men see us, what they see in us. Not potential. Not friend-ship. Just something to play with while at work, their wives and children tucked away in the safe suburban homes they pay for while at work, exposing their fantasies only to other men and the young girls they hope to trap into clandestine affairs they keep from the women they married and once loved in the same manner.

"I'm just joking, Kath. You know that, right? Here, give it back. I'll write you one for real." He reaches over the expanse of his cluttered desk and pulls it from my hands. I let him take it and watch him tear the evidence into many small scraps of paper and toss them into the garbage can beneath his desk.

"It was just a joke, okay? Are we good?" He looks into me with guarded eyes now, serious, his joke not having received the response he expected. What? A giggle? A laugh? A date to make him forget his domestic humdrum existence?

I need another job. One that does not remind me I am only a girl, a sexual girl, forced to wear skirts and femininity like a badge that provokes sexual attention from men whose letters of reference confirm her only function is her sex. Why can't I just be a girl? Why won't they just let me be a girl, left alone to just exist, to be, without constantly being told that I have one service, one purpose?

I am not my sex.

OF KNIGHTS AND VIRGINS

It is at this point that my mother begins her panoptic interrogation of me, of my body, prying my eyes open to see if my pupils are dilated, evidence of drugs; asking questions so she can identify patterns in my speech, if it is slow, slurred, evidence of alcohol. But how does she expect to discern sex on me? She can take me to a doctor to study my vagina, evidence that it is still intact. That is what parents used to do to ensure a girl's virginity had not been violated. I suppose it's in the disarray of my clothing, my buttons. Maybe the shirt untucked, gasping for air and pushing out against the stranglehold of my jeans and belt. Perhaps my buttons are not placed in the right buttonhole, or maybe there is a button missing. Something on me lets her know I have been giving it away to all the boys who want it, assuming that I want it, also, evidence that I am the whore she knew I would become when she adopted me. Just like my birth mother.

The first time it happens, I sit there shell-shocked—in the same way I stood in front of Steve as I read the sexual letter he had written for me. Both instances are humiliating, but what is even more humiliating is that I stood there—in front of him— and now I sit in front of her, a heavy weight pushing me down, pressing my feet into the floorboards, anchoring them with the same pressure pushing my tongue back, behind my tightly closed lips, jamming the words of outrage and disbelief back into my throat.

They live there, all the words I want to say, all the rage and hunger clamoring and battling for air and life and light, but they are not allowed to come out. What is this force keeping it all in there, so strong and stubborn? I think it is fear—fear of what will happen if I do say what is on my mind.

What *would* happen if I told Steve to fuck himself—or go home and fuck his wife? If I quit? If I took his letter back, before he ripped it to smithereens, and showed it to the owner of the company—or better yet, a good lawyer? If I told my mother to go fuck herself? If I refused to sit before her each time I went out and returned? What would she do? Kick me out? What then? Where would I go? How would I pay for school? How could I survive without her?

I am attached to her by the same umbilical cord she stitched between us when she first adopted me, made out of chains and barbed wire and padlocks without keys—bound to her by fear and anger and resentments and silences whose original intentions have been misplaced and are now irrevocably lost. She holds onto me and I hold onto her, but neither of us remembers why.

I think I still love her. My fear is tangled in desperation and love and this deep-seated need I have for her to accept me, to see me. It's what we all want from our parents. But even as I sit before her, only a few feet away, leaning into her, my eyes earnest and hopeful, she fails to see the girl looking back at her with longing.

"Were you drinking tonight?"

"Yes, I had a White Russian. Just one. That's all."

"Did you do drugs?"

"No." I sigh. "I don't do drugs. I would never."

"But you drink," she arches her eyes at me, as if proving to herself and to me that she has caught me in a lie.

"I had one drink. But I don't do drugs." I emphasize each word, trying not to lose control of my anger.

"Your eyes are glazed and blood-shot."

"That's because I'm tired. It's two o'clock in the morning."

Silence. Her eyes look me up and down. Every inch of me is served to her, and I cannot hide any parts of me lest she thinks I am trying to deceive her. I move my gaze to the window, watching the stars trickle like tears against the dark-blue canvas of the sky stretched out before us. I want to disappear into its fold, to be allowed to simply exist, resplendent and beautiful and bright, and to be seen, to shine and to be seen.

But I can only sit here, in front of the woman who paints the silhouette of me against a black canvas, using colors to depict me that make me feel muted and dull, until she erases all that is me so she can't find me even if she wants to. Not the real me. Not the me I want her to know and love—even if I am the me who doesn't resemble her.

"Did you have sex tonight?" Her voice clashes with my thoughts and brings me back to the couch, slapping me into the present.

"Who would I have sex with? I went to a club with Joyce and her friends. All girls."

"There are boys there."

"Yes, and where would I have sex with them?"

She only shrugs her shoulders at me.

"Ma, I'm a virgin. I haven't had sex."

"Yet. You do date a lot. You go out with different boys all the time. What do you do with them?"

"I go out on dates. That's all. I don't have sex with them."

"That's hard to believe."

"For you, maybe. But I know the truth."

"You're not always truthful."

"I am truthful. In fact, I tell you too much. And I tell you to show you that you can trust me, but I guess I'm the idiot here."

She says nothing. She just keeps looking at me as if she will find the evidence she needs to justify her suppositions if only she digs into me a little deeper, locating the niche of hidden touches and drugs and booze I keep from her.

She tires me out in places that make me feel weak and heavy, my chest rising and falling with laborious effort.

"Have you seen enough?" I ask her, readying myself to rise and go to my room, with or without her permission.

She shrugs again.

We sit opposite each other for a few more minutes, staring at each other. She's waiting for me to say something. What? I don't know what she wants from me, and I don't ask. Eventually, I muster enough courage to move out of the frame of her gaze, walk past her, and head to my room, where I toss my weary limbs onto my bed, the worn-out mattress catching my blind fall, cradling me in its wrinkled center, and I sink into it without resistance—with relief, really.

The interrogations of my body become recurring, like bad dreams I surrender to because I don't have the strength or wherewithal to wake myself out of them. I participate with the movements of a sleepwalker, detouring my legs to the right as I enter the apartment, sitting opposite her as if I am a guest in her home, on her plastic-covered couch, receiving unraveling eye-stares instead of coffee or tea.

And I take it. I take it like a victim because I don't know what else to do. Because she is my bread and butter. Because she hasn't seen me yet, and I know that deep down, she loves me, and one day, she will see me. She shames me because she loves me. She accuses me because she loves me. I sit for her as one does for a painter, still and mute, waiting for the moment she will release me and I can shake off the sensation of being exposed—naked and wanting—to the assumptions and judgments of others. I sit for her because I love her in the twisted way she has taught me all about love, the kind of love that is sure to entangle me with the wrong kind of man, the one who wants to own me, control me, suppress me—in all the ways she does and in many other ways I am not aware of yet. The ways of lovers, perhaps.

I tremble at the idea of finding the kind of love I am learning from her in men. Maybe this is why I am so afraid to commit, why I am still a virgin. If I surrender to these interrogations out of love, how will I behave towards a man who will treat me the same way? What if I find one just like her, and I love him because he won't give me what I need from him: unconditional love, respect, decency? In escaping her, what if I end up right back here, sitting in front of a man shaming me, cursing me, loving me with controlled words and controlling hands?

I shake off the thoughts and return to the last four hours of the night I spent with Christian.

Christian of Castlecore. A knight I meet in my medieval literature course at Queens.

He sits next to me, and we begin writing notes to each other. He looks a lot like my John from Cancun, dark hair, solid built, tanned hands with curly wisps of hair I want to tangle my fingers into and pull oh so lightly. Again, I am surprised that this guy wants to talk to me. He sends me notes during class and laughs at my responses aloud, garnering the attention of our middle-aged professor who continues with his lectures on Arthurian tradition while casting us disapproving glances for not paying attention. We meet for coffee during the week and talk about the Green Knight in one of our short stories, and he watches me quietly while I ramble on about how much I love the idea of knights in armor and ladies in medieval gowns and the honor code with which the men shrouded their women.

"You know, I'm a knight," he confesses one day.

"Ya, right." I laugh at him.

"No, seriously. I work at a medieval fair in Long Island, and I have the knight's armor and gear and everything. If you go out with me, I'll show it to you. We have to make our own costumes, too."

I look at him, and he nods in earnest, making a cross along his chest with his fingers to show me his seriousness. "That is so cool. I've never met a knight before."

"Well, if you go out with me, you can say that you even dated one." He winks, and I have to suppress a giggle.

He takes me to Pizzeria Uno and then to his apartment in Corona, where he wants to show me his knight's armor. He lives in the basement of a home in a quiet suburban street, and as soon as we enter his home, he runs to the closet and pulls out his gear. There is the iron mask, the plate armor, the sword, the cape, and when I ask him to put it all on, he says, no way. It's all too heavy. He shows me his family's crest and the name he has chosen for it. Christian of Castlecore.

Christian of Castlecore has a mirror in his room. On his ceiling. A long, wide, massive mirror that parallels the length and width of his queen-sized bed. He doesn't point it out to me but I make a mental note of it when I follow him into his room so he can tuck his suit of armor back into his closet. I laugh when I see the mirror. A nervous kind of laugh that shows my discomfort.

He looks at me then. Quietly. Assessing my reaction, I'm sure, so I try to hide my blush and adopt the glib attitude I believe I have mastered.

"That's a big mirror," I point to it, avoiding looking at his bed, wondering what kind of girls he lies with on it, what kind of girls like watching him and themselves having sex. I mean, that's what it's there for, right? I'm not that naive, but for the first time, I'm a little taken aback, unsure of what he will expect from me, a guy with a mirror on his ceiling, over his bed.

But he takes my hand instead and leads me out of the room, guiding me to the couch in his small living room.

"You know, sometimes I just like watching myself in bed." He moves the bangs away from my face and searches my eyes with his.

"Uh huh," is all I can manage. He just smiles at me with open amusement, his dimples dancing to the rhythm of the soft chuckle I hear under his breath.

He's tender, with a balance of sweetness and masculinity all tumbling out of him at once, and when he moves in for a kiss, I purr like a satisfied cat before our lips even meet. His tongue sweeps past my lips and explores my insides, leaving the taste of nicotine to linger on my gums and teeth as his mouth continues to move to my cheek, my eyelids, my chin. I straddle him on the couch and am fascinated by the fact that an hour passes with us kissing—and only kissing—his hands never taking detours or in- direct turns to parts of me I won't let him touch. He doesn't even try to fondle my chest, his fingers locked in my hair as he tastes me with the same kind of investment I taste him. We are one kiss, one beautiful, pure, long, lovely kiss, unencumbered by fear or unspoken expectations. I am a lady, minus the straddling part, and he is my knight in shining armor, taking only what I give him—my mouth, my hair in his fingers, my thighs resting securely, safely, on his, his hands remaining in safe zones the entire time.

He makes me feel so good and so protected that I want to kiss him like this forever. Without pushy, roving hands inter- rupting the succor I nestle into when I am in his mouth and he is in mine. It's the most exquisite, delightful feeling in the world, kissing without fear of what comes next, knowing that Christian has already decided I am not the mirror kind of girl. It is nice to be seen by a guy, being kissed with a reverence that feels like floating on my back, resting my head on the lapping waters of a calm lake, my limbs gliding on the surface of gentle waves that lap across my shoulders and neck without submerging me or making me struggle for my bearing or forcing me to cough up salt water that all but drowns me.

This is our one and only date, though, and I don't see him again for the rest of the semester. He doesn't return to our class, and I sit in the back, next to his empty chair wondering where he is, if I did something wrong or said something stupid to chase him away. He kissed me. He held my hand. He respected my boundaries, knew them without me identifying them to him, so where did I go wrong? I succumb to dry lectures about knights wondering where mine had gone.

But after a few weeks, he calls me again. Through the line,

his voice is kind, sweet, husky, but he doesn't answer my questions as to his whereabouts. Eventually, I put him on the list of the stupid boys who snip pieces of my heart and squander them as if what's left is going to restore itself, transform into a whole heart where there isn't much left to begin with. I let his voice find root in my answering machine until he also gives up, knowing I will no longer take his calls.

Many boys, long kisses, persistent hands, and a year later, I feel his eyes resting on me at Malibu's, my favorite dance club situated along the shorelines of Long Island's Lido Beach. My White Russian already ingested, its numbing effects slithering along my chin and the tips of my fingers, I dance in a circle with Joyce, Helen, and Liz, feeling the pull of him as if we are attached to each other by some kind of invisible rope, and I turn to look for him. When my eyes find him, he's sitting on the middle of a bunch of tiered steps, watching me, the softness of his look caressing me without words. I move to him, our eyes locked, as if I am headed home, back to my knight.

"Christian of Castlecore," I murmur when he reaches out and takes me into his arms. I am mesmerized, in part by my drink and in part by the musky scent of his cologne and sweat, navigating me back to the memory of the long and enveloping kisses we had shared the year before.

"Go out with me," he yells in my ear, over the club music, his lips soft and wet on my lobe, his breath causing my knees to buckle beneath me, a long sinewy chill crawling up my spine, tingling the pores on my scalp.

"Maybe," I say weakly, but already know I will. My body remembers being held by him, my mouth waters at the memory of his kisses, and I want to be kissed like that again, to fall into the hunger of a boy's mouth without being ravaged by his wants. I wonder if he still kisses this way. I want to know him again.

That was a week ago. Tonight, the night of my interrogation, is the night we go out for the first time since our first rendezvous at his apartment a year ago. This time, however, we keep it local, driving to a Greek restaurant in Forest Hills. While crossing the street from the parking lot, I grab his hand to pull him from entering the intersection as a red Corvette makes a fast and blind turn towards us. He stops short and looks at me as if seeing me for the first time. He curls his fingers into mine and we walk the rest of the way to the restaurant along the busy Metropolitan Avenue lined with shops, cars, and restaurants of all kinds.

Sitting opposite him, I am nervous and warm, my hands and insides fluttering like butterflies unable to fly a straight path in the air, looking for a gnarled branch to land and hold on to for support, for something solid to hold us still.

"I like the way you did that," he begins, taking my hand in his and fingering the intersecting lines on my clammy palm. I have the urge to take it back and wipe it along the fabric of my jeans, but I don't want to disturb the moment and will my heart to stop pounding in my ears instead.

"Did what?" I ask, confusion furrowing my brows.

"The way you grabbed my hand. It felt so protective. So caring." His hazel eyes cling to mine, making me aware for the first time that opposite me sits a boy who is perhaps looking for the same things I am. Love. Tenderness. Care.

"That's because I do care about you. You're a nice person," I tell him, gulping down my Coke, the sweet liquid cooling the fires continuing to rise in me.

Then a thought dawns on me.

"Doesn't anyone hold your hand?"

"I just broke up with this girl. She stopped holding my hand," he reveals, his eyes boring into mine for a response. "And anyway, she never grabbed it with such protectiveness as you did. I just never met a girl like you before."

"That's odd. I love holding hands. It's the nicest part of being with someone."

"I get that about you. And I get that you like kissing, too." His grin widens and I meet his dimples again.

"I love kissing," I admit. "Sometimes I wish that's all that existed. Just kissing, pure and beautiful." I don't know what makes me say this, except I trust him. And I know that we will kiss at the end of the night. I want to fast-forward to that moment and leave all this behind me, but I also like sitting opposite him, having him reveal his own vulnerabilities, realizing that beneath the knight and the boy who kisses me with tenderness lies another human being with his own set of needs.

When he drives me home, he parks his jeep a block away from my mother's apartment. He unbuckles his seatbelt, then mine, pushes his seat back, and then scoops me onto his lap so I am sitting on him sideways. Locking my arms around him, I turn my face to his, and the kiss is everything I have anticipated, everything I remember and more. It is long and deep and soul-searching, our lips talking to each other in another language, revealing aches and truths we don't reveal to anyone else. We kiss for an hour, longer even, until the windows of his jeep are foggy from our heated breathing. My cheeks and chin are red, burned from the stubble of his goatee as it rubs against my skin, and I love knowing that when I go home, I will still have evidence of him on me.

This is the only evidence my mother finds on me as she stares me up and down, but I don't care that my skin is raw or that she can see it. I escape into thoughts of him as she surveys my body, the memory of his mouth on me still burning my flesh like the dying embers of a fading brushfire.

There are no buttons unhooked or shirt twisted and inside out for her to discover. He doesn't touch me under my clothes or even on top of my clothes. He caresses the length of my neck with his fingertips and lips, leaving a trail of wet kisses on my skin that burn and birth an ache in me. He pulls my hair back to taste my collarbone with his mouth, but he goes no further than kissing, almost as if he knows exactly what I want, giving me just that and only that. He is a giver, and he gives without demanding anything in return.

And I take because it is a good, harmless kind of wanting. A wanting that cradles and devours at the same time, making me feel safe in love—in this kind of impermanence that won't last past the night. I recognize myself in him. He is as transient as I am, looping in and out of people's lives, searching for a missing part of himself without knowing which part it is that he has lost or misplaced, hoping the next girl he finds will offer it to him, fit into him in the way that he needs.

I savor his offerings, his lips on mine, his hands interlocked with my own, his scent on my skin. And as I walk to my door, looking over my shoulder only once, for just a quick glance at him, I know I won't see him again. There is a sadness in him that I touched only for a second when I grabbed his hand and pulled him onto the curb—a sadness that brings him to me and then pulls him away again. I don't have the words he needs to hear from me, to make him stay, to bring him back to me. I'm not experienced in the language of other people's loneliness. I am only well-versed in my own, so I watch him drive off, I let him go, and I hope that this loose thread that dangles between us will tighten and bring us back together again. Somewhere. Somehow. Because he is my tender knight. My Christian of Castlecore.

THE BROKEN VIRGIN

"*Putana*," my mother's voice scrapes against the rigid lines of my back. Her head is sticking out of our apartment window, and I wonder if she is not embarrassed that someone might see her, hear her, align her with the young whore walking down the street to Joyce's house dressed in jeans, combat boots, and a red and black checkered flannel shirt over a black, loose-fitting tank top. Her words clamor and clash against the iron-clad barriers I have constructed around me that mute her, render her powerless in diminishing what is left of my virtues.

Perhaps I am the whore she sees in me. After all, I have had my share of alcohol, I go to dance clubs and bars at least three nights a week, and I have had my bra unhooked, my breasts fondled, and my hips ground into the bulging hips of a few boys with whom I've dated up to three months. But this is the cutoff. Still. They lose patience with me way before that, or I dump them as soon they mention their blue balls, which I find crude and tasteless. I don't know what will happen after the third month. John, the first one, is the only one who lasted three months. Maybe this is why three months is a breaking point for me. Everything seems to sour around that time, and I hold onto my virginity even tighter, like a life vest keeping me afloat in a treacherous sea of raging waves and emaciated sharks with a hankering for the blood between my thighs.

I am twenty-three now, starting my first year of graduate school at Queens College. I have decided to teach literature on the high school level. I still live at home and still work two jobs to pay for my graduate tuition, which is more expensive now. I still sit down on the couch each time I come home from a night out with friends or from a date so my mother can inspect me as she would a cluster of bacteria under a microscope looking for the answers to her own misgivings—whatever they are—which she withholds from me as if there's a dark secret in me that will taint and disrupt her existence if it ever comes out.

She is still a mystery to me, but I have grown tired of trying to solve her. I can only work on myself, and this is what I do. I do it well. I am single-minded, an automaton. I go to work during the day, to school at night, to work and dance clubs on the weekends. I meet Shirley, another graduate student at Queens enrolled in the Big Buddy for Homeless Kids program. She and I take our girls out together, and since Shirley has a car, it is easier to get around when we decide to stay in Queens.

We pick up our girls from a homeless shelter a few blocks in from Queens Boulevard in Kew Gardens. My girl's name is Jazmin. She is twelve years old, Puerto Rican, and quiet. It's hard to get a word out of her, but thanks to Shirley, who is half-Jewish and half-Puerto Rican, she is able to cut through the shy shell that shrouds this little girl. Our job is to expose them to culture, give them a mentor to look up to, encourage them to trust in their education, and journal about our experiences. I do this not just for the A I will receive each semester this year or because it will look good on my resume when I apply for a teaching job—

although these are some of the reasons. I do it because everything in my life up to this point is about me. My work, my trou-
bles, my virginity, my education. I want to do something for
someone else, to give a girl with an unstable home and circumstances something solid, something fun that will ground her, to
get her out of the homeless shelter environment she is trapped in
because her parents can't afford the American Dream coming
here promised them.

Jazmin has a little sister who is eight years old, and she tells
me she can use a break from her as well. I don't know what it's
like to grow up with siblings—only my mother—and although
our life is quiet, it's an insufferable kind of quiet that strangles
and chokes with unvoiced expectations hunched between us,
equally silent but thriving, breathing heavily down my neck. I'm
glad to give Jazmin the chance to get out, to see the city, to go to
the Metropolitan Museum of Art, to go ice-skating, or just to
grab ice-cream and lick sweetness while riding the train to the
congested part of Queens we both call our home.

My favorite part of the program is Shirley. It's very hard for
me to make friends. I'm not good at small talk and I don't hang
out with girls I don't know on a casual basis. Shirley and I become friends in this easy manner that feels something like drap-
ing softened butter on a bagel. That seamless. That smooth and
satisfying. There is no labor involved, no undue effort.

"Let's take the girls out together," she offers the first time we
meet, and I am grateful to her. Although I go through the application and interview process to get into the program without
overthinking it, both Jazmin and I are shy, and Shirley's offer
lightens the load of getting to know a stranger with whom I
don't have much in common—not to mention that she's a kid.

For someone like me, who lives very much inside her head, coming out to talk to someone I don't know is a laborious effort, a burden, and I run scripted lines and questions in my head to say aloud to the girl who finds no issue with sitting next to me without saying a word, comfortable in our silences, confident in her skin.

Shirley frees me of this burden. She makes me laugh, her blond hair brushing against the smooth line of her shoulders. There is one incident when we're driving along some busy intersection in Queens and her teenaged buddy tosses a paper bag out of the back-seat car window.

"Oh, hell no!" The words fly out of her mouth and her foot slams on the brake, pulling us to a sudden stop. "You get out right now and pick your trash up. You will not litter the streets with your trash." The girl refuses to get out of the car. We are in the middle of the road, so Shirley gets out, picks it up, and gives it back to the girl, who places it on her lap and looks disgraced.

I sit beside Shirley, laughing in this silent but deep way where only heavy breaths come out. No sound. I love her. She says what is on her mind, she is cool and confident and pretty, and I am surprised she's hanging out with me—of all people. The quiet, serious, brown-haired, brown-eyed girl who hugs corners and lurks in the shadows of others. She pulls me out of the shadows, makes me laugh, calls me on Thursday nights to see if I want to go to a bar—she'll pick me up. She does not know I am hungover with depression, my entire body weighed down by loneliness, a possessive lover who overpowers me, climbs on top of me and shoves my head face first into my pillow until my breath weakens and fades, letting go only when my limbs are numb and still beneath his force.

As soon as the invitation is out of her mouth, I wriggle out of his grasp, grab my things, and flee from the dark grip of my room, out of the apartment, out of the house and all the darkness it possesses. I wait for her outside where the air pushes into me through my pores and shakes me back to life. It's only when I am sitting beside her, nestled in the passenger side of her car, a mile away from my home, that I feel relief and heady with the taste of freedom. Like licorice. Like childhood unencumbered by adults or their dysfunction.

Whereas my other friends, Joyce, Helen, and Diana take me dancing on Friday and Saturday nights, my Thursday nights with Shirley involve drinking at a bar and talking about *Melrose Place* and *90201*, television shows we watch before she calls me to go out. I limit myself to one White Russian and drink it until I feel my chin go numb. I stop drinking then. I don't like hangovers when I drink too much. I don't like when I drink so much that I black out.

It's happened twice, both times at Malibu's with my girlfriends to care for me, but still. The idea of blacking out scares me. It scares me to think of what can happen to me, my body, without me being conscious of any of it. Without me remembering any of it. I take such good care and control of my body, my sex, and then to lose that control, the rights to my self-ownership, my voice to consent or not to consent going out the window and never remembering it is unfathomable to me. Unforgivable. I don't know that I would ever forgive myself for this kind of weakness, this kind of foolishness, carelessness with the one body I have been given to treat with respect and kindness.

The first time I black out, I down a pink, fruity shot from the bar after Barbara, Joyce's friend, shows her boobs to the bartender for free shots. One minute I am walking away from the bar towards the dance floor, and the next minute, I wake up making out with this guy I wouldn't normally be kissing if sober. I've been dancing with him, near him, for the past two years, but we have never exchanged names or numbers. And here I am, kissing him. I mean, it isn't bad. The kiss. He just isn't my type with his grungy long red hair and pierced ears, nose, and lip. I like clean-cut guys with stubble and goatees. I like knights.

Coming to while kissing him makes it awkward to dance around him afterwards with no mention of what we have done. I don't even think he is into me like this—he has never asked me out in all the years we've danced together and have said no more to each other than "Hey!"

The second—and last time—I am so fried, I come to while vomiting in a bag in the back seat of Helen's Acura Integra. I don't even remember the night, having drunk too much Vodka and Snapple in the bathroom stall we all share inside the club—in addition to my usual White Russian. Apparently, one of the bouncers had to carry me to Helen's car, and Helen and Joyce laugh the entire way home. Joyce, the party mom, pushes my hair back from my sticky face and makes me hold the bag in front of my mouth. Full of vomit, I take it with me upstairs and into my room. It is four in the morning, so my mother has not waited up to interrogate me on this night. But the next afternoon, when I return home from my eight-hour shift at the TV rental company, I can't find my bag of vomit. She doesn't say a word to me, and I don't bring it up either. It is a subject better off hissing quietly among all the other remnants of conversations that pile up unvoiced between us.

From this point on, one White Russian has been enough. I

don't like being out of control, but I do enjoy the numbness that courses through me after a few sips of my favorite milk and Kahlua drink, making me feel loopy but aware, watching people around me from a hazy distance. This numbness washes away the weight that has found permanent residence on my shoulders, curving my back slightly so that if I am not aware of it, I take on the look of a hunched girl, a broken girl.

My friendships lighten the load I carry. Shirley and Joyce and Helen and Diana. They become the girls with whom I share my secrets, my hopes, my losses. We drink, we dance, but we talk, too. We are all young women searching for love and passion at night, single-mindedly pursuing careers during the day. Joyce gets a job as a manager at an office supply store. Diana becomes a social worker. Shirley, a guidance counselor. Helen, a CPA in the big city. And me, I begin my student teaching internship at Flushing High School while pursuing my master's in Secondary Education. We are driven, we work, we laugh and cry and complain about guys, and we party, looking out for each other—like the time I blacked out and they all took charge of me—of the body I obsessively protect from male hands and prying eyes. I feel love for them, and I am loved by them.

What I don't get from them, I find in the guys I date, and I date a lot. Whereas my friends go from boyfriend to boyfriend, I go from date to date. It is rare for me to date the same guy a second time, and I watch them with their boyfriends, the way they connect, the intimacy they share that I have yet to possess with another human being—a male human being—and yearning burns through me like a destructive fire that is out of control.

"Kath," Helen laughs at me. "You change guys with the same frequency we all change our underwear."

"Ew!" I whine, smacking her shoulder as she drives us to Malibu's, speeding along the Long Island Expressway towards the beach. "Gross analogy."

Helen went to middle school with Joyce, and I met her through Joyce, but she has become one of my favorite friends. She is tall and Chinese, her slim, long body a seductive attraction for most guys. She is beautiful and fun, and we have a lot of drunken experiences we laugh over. She is free and experimental with guys and sex in the way that I am the opposite, holding them off, pushing them off, shutting down any thoughts of sexual pleasure that may be assumed when they see me dancing with my friends. I am not open in this way, and perhaps this is what I like about her. That she is liberated but that she is also the smartest girl I know—a perfectly packaged girl with brains and sex appeal and niceness to boot. I cannot help but be protective of her, though, because I see how guys watch her, and sometimes I have to push them away, disgusted by the arousal I witness them licking off their lips as they fantasize about her—a girl they do not know.

"It's just sex, Kath," she says as if it's nothing. She likes the way they look at her, the way they grind their hips towards her on the dance floor, crushing her with their desire. But where she sees just sex, I see sexual objectification. I see hungry wolves using her for one thing only—her sex, her body—without wanting to know the Helen this finely chiseled body belongs to, the smart and sweet girl I know and love.

"You have one body. You should use it with care and share it only with people you care for and who will care for it—your body," I tell her.

But I know she thinks I am too conservative. I'm a virgin.

What do I know about the pleasures of the body? I've never even had an orgasm, asking friends about what it feels like, what makes it so wonderful everyone around me seeks it out with blind determination.

"How do you know she's having an orgasm?" I ask my friend Joe about his girlfriend.

He's been dating the same girl for the past two years, and we both know she gets angry when he and I hang out without her. We're just friends, he tells her, but she doesn't believe him. Whenever we hang out as a group, I try my best to befriend her, but I am a threat. I don't like Joe that way. He's only my friend, my best friend for years now, having gone through my break with John during our first year of college. When I am lonely or heartbroken, he is there, an Asian guy with spiky black hair, driving me along Queens Boulevard or Bell Boulevard in his black Camaro, taking me to shoot pool or just to sit somewhere for coffee and talk about love and our ambitions. As much as I love him as a friend, my stomach muscles don't clench with desire in all the years we've been friends, and when we lie on the hood of his car looking up at the stars flickering against the night sky, our arms touching, there is nothing more between us except the kind of easy love that doesn't trickle into the tolerant hues of our friendship. No lines are ever blurred between us, and I know I can tell him anything and he won't mock me or try to use it to his advantage. There is beauty and kindness in a friendship with a boy who makes a girl feel safe and untrodden upon.

We're talking about his girlfriend now, Carolyn. "I just know." He laughs at me, at my naivety.

"Yeah, but how do you know she's not faking it?" I know about this faking from books, movies, and television shows that depict women who, because they don't want to hurt their partner's feelings, sigh, lie beneath them, and count the spider webs they discover on the ceilings above their bed as the men pump in and out of their bodies, grunting, unconcerned with the fact that the women they invade—their lovers, the ones they love— are not into it in a most obvious way. I know about orgasms from my friends who tell me over drinks or between dances or as we're sitting in the car waiting for one or the other to finish their hookup with a guy, getting a number or prolonging a drunken kiss.

"I just know," he tells me. "Anyway, you'll find out when you do it. You'll see. It's great—better than great. When it's good, it's amazing, and you want it more and more. Like a drug."

"Could you just tell me how you know she's having one? What are the signs?"

"Her entire body shakes, trembles. She has these uncontrollable spasms, and I just know she's not faking it."

I frown. I'm not fully satisfied with this answer, but I guess I will have to wait to experience it for myself.

I'm almost twenty-four, and I haven't had one yet. Not only do I not let guys touch me below my belly button but neither do I. I don't touch myself. I don't have the desire or the know-how and I'm not curious enough to want to know. In fact, I have begun wearing onesies, like a baby.

They look like one-piece bathing suits that snap at the crotch, and I call them my virginity armor, or my no-access shirts. I wear them on dates because they look good with my tight jeans but also because it makes it hard for guys when they do try to get past the waistband of my jeans. And they do. Try to. To no avail. When my hands tire of pushing them off, my no-access shirts most definitely do the job. They tire of kissing and grinding and fighting me for access, and this is when the dates usually end. Some guys try for another date, but most give up right there and then. There are easier girls out there. Not me. You don't know me. You don't get me. And you most definitely do not get into my pants or anywhere else in that region.

I know only the pleasures of the kiss, and I kiss often. For now, I want only the pleasures of the mouth on my mouth. Each mouth, each pair of lips, each boy's kiss is different, tastes differently, burns with various intensities, makes different parts of my body shift and tingle, and kissing becomes a way of me getting to know my own body, how it moves, how it trembles, how it melts and sways.

Who knows? Maybe if I do have sex, I will want it more, and I will want it from more than one guy. But the idea makes me cringe and my fingers itch to curl into themselves, my nails digging into the palms of my hands, leaving their warning marks behind.

It's not who I am. I don't want a lot of guys. I want one. One who will know me and love me and wait for me. And this is okay, too. I am about control. Not experience and pleasure. I can wait for both. I can wait for the one who will wait with me, love the me that is not attached to the body and curves that belong to me irrespective of who I am inside. It is just sex. Loving me is harder, takes more effort, more commitment. It takes more than one or two dates. It sure as hell takes longer than three months and "I love you" phrases intended to fuck me.

I will wait for as long as it takes to fall in love and be loved. Even if it takes forever. In the meantime, I date. I kiss. A lot. Kissing is like sipping White Russians—when I'm kissing the right guy, of course. The best kisses leave me heady, woozy, and with my eyes closed I am floating on the wings of butterflies fluttering beneath me to the rhythm of the blood pumping in my chest, aching, pulsing against my ribcage for release that only comes when the next boy places his lips on mine and I lick the longing on him that echoes my own.

My longing sits quietly beside me as my mother stares at my body. She squirms in her seat, feeling as uncomfortable as I used to feel when this invasion began. I am numb to it, to my mother. I sit before her still and absent, the same way I sat while on my violin teacher's lap while his hands scanned over my bare shoulders, waist, and back. I wish she could see my longing instead, on the verge of tears, my heart breaking with every knowing nod my mother makes, a demonstration of her knowledge of me, her awareness of my sins. And what is this unforgettable, unforgiveable sin, anyway? The knowledge that my birth mother was a *putana*. A prostitute. My low birth means I will return to it as if it is a flaw absorbed by my DNA. Not a choice.

One day, my longing punches me in the arm, nudging me out of my stupor, my obedience. I rise from the couch and walk out of the living room, past my mother.

"I'm not done with you," she insists, trying to gather the control I have taken from her as if they are scraps of loose paper I have torn and tossed into her face. She rushes towards me. I turn into the hallway bathroom and attempt to close the door, but she pushes her shoulders into it and pulls it away from my grasp. I face the mirror, looking at myself, and I can see her from my peripheral vision. We're both looking at me now, the dark marks under my eyes, the bangs that need trimming, the unsmiling mouth that only feels light when lips brush up against it, coaxing love into me.

"Look at you," she begins. "You look old already and you're only in your twenties. You're going to turn out just like your mother."

I hate when this mother brings up the original mother, the one who sold herself for money, who broke my family into jagged shards of glass, separated from their foundation, and given away as if they were scraps of clothing for the taking. If I can't talk about her, then why does Ann? What right does she have?

But I don't say any of this. All I can muster is my rage.

"Fuck you!" I breathe heavily into the mirror, my watery, wasted eyes clashing with hers through the glass.

Before I can say anything else, her hand reaches out toward me and she slaps me in the face. Everything goes dark in me. Without thinking or planning, I move one step in her direction, grab her by the throat, and pull her into the tiny bathroom. My knuckles still tight, shaking, grind deeper into her neck skin, and I shove her head against the mirror so that the gray hairs on her scalp loosen and cling to the mirror's surface. Her eyes, small, beady, brown look at me with fear, and there is a part of me that likes it. I am now in control, in charge, except it's not my eyes that are locking her in place. It's my hand, and I squeeze just a bit more to see her eyes widen, her fear tremble with the knowledge of my power.

I bring my face close to hers, no longer diffident and unsure. "If you hit me one more time, it will come right back at you. Do you understand me?"

I don't wait for her to respond. I loosen my grip from her throat and walk away from her. Once in my room, I slam the door shut and fall on my bed, exhausted, trembling. This isn't me; I don't hurt people. I don't use force. Guilt surfaces, and for the first time since I rose from my seat on the couch during her investigation of me, I am afraid. Afraid of the punishment I will have to face.

But no punishment comes. Only silence. Our existence in our small apartment is wordless, quiet, uneasy in its stillness. When she passes me in the hallway, she hugs the wall, afraid of me, her eyes hanging low, her mouth gripped tightly against her face. There is a scarf wrapped around her throat, and once—just once—she makes sure to remove it so I can see the black and blue marks my fingers left behind, evidence of my violence, my wayward roots. Roots that don't come from her. That she is not responsible for since I have not emerged from her womb.

I know I should leave. But I don't. Fear and love and longing keep me chained to her as if she is the source of my survival.

I stay. And it all goes back to the way it's been between us. Except I never sit on the couch again, her eyes prying me open for the taking. Never again.

ONE LONELY VIRGIN

For the next year, I date a lot. I kiss a whole lot more. My heart breaks again and again, and I spend many nights curled into a lonely little ball on my bed, trying to mute the sounds of my sobs from my mother's ears. Waiting for the right guy is a lonely business, a waiting game that most often feels like there is something wrong with me.

I stand in front of the mirror to search for evident flaws. I am thin, small, with curves that my jeans and shirts crowd over, hugging my breasts and taut stomach with a tight embrace. I have dark brown hair that I have begun to highlight, choppy bangs covering my forehead and falling into dark, big, chestnut-shaped eyes. I line my lips with shades of brown and this is the only makeup I put on my face. Wide-rimmed glasses rest on the slight bridge of my nose, standing between me and eyes that have to go through glass to look into mine, like citadels guarding a city's most cherished possessions from becoming spoils of war and despair. My glasses protect me from onlookers, or, at least, they make me feel less seen, and I walk through crowded dance floors at Malibu's or Webster Hall with my spine straight and my feet as if they belong and know the route on which they lead the rest of me.

Boys come in and out of my life as if a revolving door stands between us, forcing them to enter and then leave the same way while I sit on my cushy chair and watch them, the door ushering the next one towards me without a hiccup. Or maybe I am the one moving through the revolving door. Who knows? It's all a blur. One boy after another. One kiss after another. One breakup after another.

There's Rocky. He's a burly Italian who lives in Brooklyn. With dark hair and dark eyes, he's dumb as nails, but I go out with him anyway. He's a good kisser and the first guy who tries to sneak his fingers in my pants. Literally trying to get in my pants. I don't let him, of course, and neither do my onesies. The one he struggles with has a red-wine velvety fabric he traces with his fingertips, watching me as they trail lower and lower from the covered tips of my breasts, as if I am going to let him. We've only been dating a month, and I laugh when he tells me he loves me and wants to introduce me to his parents. I meet his parents, but I don't love him. Not after a month of dating. Not when he thinks words of love will win him parts of me untouched by any boy's rushed and earnest hands. What does it mean for them to touch me there? Do they think the next step is sex? I am growing impatient. Angry. And I lose it one night when Rocky calls me.

"Hey, so your mom called me yesterday," he lets me know.

"What? How'd she get your number?" I sit on the edge of my bed because my knees are shaking.

"It doesn't matter. I actually wasn't home. She ended up talking to my mother, and my mother told me about their conversation." His voice was matter of fact.

"What the fuck!" I want to find her, stick my finger in her face, and yell at her. But I lie down on my bed, wallowing into it. I don't get her. Why does she call my friends and boyfriends? When will this end? "Why did she call you?"

"Basically, she asked my mom to ask me not to keep you out so late. You have work and school, and it's not nice to have you out so late. She has a point. I think I dropped you off at two thirty in the morning the other day."

I nearly scoff at this but hold back my disdain. He wasn't complaining that night while we were steaming up the windows in his car, his fingers attempting to unbuckle my jeans.

"Listen," he said, "it's not a big deal. My mom agrees, too. We'll just make sure to get you back home early. When you go out with your friends, you should do that, too."

"Excuse me?" I can't control the coldness in my tone. He is pissing me off. Even more than my mother.

"Kathy, you know you get home way too late when you go out with your friends. I mean seriously, maybe you should cut down on the partying a bit. I mean, you have me now. You don't need to party so much."

"Are you fucking serious?" I sit up on my bed. Where was this guy a few nights ago when we were kissing and hanging out?

"And you curse too much. Nice girls don't curse."

"How about this for a nice girl," I gather up the nerve to retort. "Why don't you go fuck yourself?" With this, I hang up the phone, my hands trembling. I don't pick up when it rings again and again. I don't need a macho guy telling me what to do. Especially one who's okay doing what he's doing to me and then decides he wants to control me by dictating what time I get home. I already have a mother, thank you.

"Asshole," I spit at the phone, feeling a thrill of pleasure at the idea of him getting pissed off with every ring that is not addressed.

Then there's Ron. Ron is another Italian guy but he's older.

In his early thirties. I meet him through a group of friends, and even though I don't date older men—and guys in their thirties are too old for me—I find myself attracted to his genuine manners. I meet him at a club in the Hamptons and we hit if off immediately. Completely. He reminds me a lot of my John from Cancun. He looks a lot like him: older, mature, dark hair cut short, muscles bulging out of his shirt, hazel eyes that probe with gentleness and understanding. I spend the entire time we're at the club with him, and by the end of the evening, we are kissing—a long intimate kiss that is sweeter, more endearing than passionate. His mouth is not rushed or impatient on my skin, my lips, capturing my tongue with confidence, not possession. His hands stay in my hair, my chin, my high cheekbones, hands that echo experience but also tenderness. I realize for the first time how much I miss this kind of touch—tenderness. I've only found it with a few guys—John from Cancun, Horacio from Cancun, Christian of Castlecore, and now Ron from Florida—and yet these are the same guys who disappear like early morning mist once the sun rises. They flicker in and flicker out with the assurance of dying embers, leaving me behind in gray smoke that snakes into my lungs and chokes me temporarily—until they're gone. Just like that.

Because he lives in Florida, we stay in touch, and every time he visits, we meet up. Usually, it's at Malibu's, and we pick up where we left off the last time we had seen each other. Kissing him again is like kissing him for the first time. We do this for about a year, seeing each other three or four times. In between, we both see other people. At least I do. He's in Florida. I'm in New York. I'm in my early twenties. I'm not settling into the impermanence of a long-distance relationship.

"What's your favorite kind of car?" he asks me between sips of beer and kisses.

"Ah," I smile at him, wishing I could fold him up like a dollar bill and tuck him into my pocket. "I don't know. I'm not into cars. I don't even have one."

"How do you get around?"

"Public transportation mostly. But my friends have cars when we go to the Hamptons or anywhere in Long Island. Otherwise, I can get around easily via trains and buses."

"You know I own a car dealership, right?"

"Uh huh," I nod my head, reaching out to place a small, quick kiss on his lips, tasting the beer remnants he hasn't licked off yet.

"I can get you any car you want. Just tell me which one." He kisses me back, running his long, slender fingers through my hair, deftly combing through my knots without causing me any discomfort. A sigh of pleasure passes through my lips and he catches it with another kiss. "What do you think?" he asks when I don't respond.

"I don't need a car. I don't even have a license, but even if I did, I wouldn't take a car from you."

"But I want to give you one. I like you so much. I think about you all the time. I can't get you out of my head. I want to show you how much you mean to me. Let me gift you one." My body grows cold, and I pull away from his hands, his lips, putting a few feet of distance between us.

He notices the shift in my demeanor. "I'm not trying to insult you. I'm sorry if I have. I just really like you. This is the only way I know how to show you my feelings for you."

"Look, I don't want a car. If you want to do something nice

for me, then keep kissing me, keep calling me, keep seeing me when you're in town. That's enough for me."

He shakes his head at me, his eyes soft, sincere, the warmth I find there wrapped around me like a blanket that keeps the cold out. "Most girls would take a free car without hesitation," he says quietly, his fingers finding their home back in my hair. Even the brown tresses on my head sigh with pleasure at his touch.

"Not me. I have no use for a car. And," I add after a few seconds, "that is an extravagant gift to give someone you don't know all that well."

"I know you," he whispers in my ear, leaving a flurry of tingles that propel me closer to his solid chest, my hands sliding up his arms and finding a comfortable spot to rest on his shoulders, my body nestling against the length of his. He's like a big comfy bed I want to curl into like a baby ready for a midday nap, surrendering to sleep with a satisfied and contented smile plastered onto my face. "And that's why I want to give you everything. I think I can love you. A part of me already does. I can see living my life with you, growing old with you." He pauses long enough to look into my face for a response. "Does this scare you?"

I shake my head.

"No," I lie. My insides tense and shiver at the prospect. I'm not ready for this, my inner voice shrieks with fear. And as he leans in for another kiss, a longer one this time, one that echoes the intensity of his words, I feel parts of me peeling away from him, the important parts, the heart, the thoughts, the nerves, the muscles—the rest of me—skin and bones—still resting against him out of desperation, trying to absorb the energy and steel will I need to let go all the way—all of me away from all of him—his sweet kindness and his silly words of love for a girl he doesn't know—he can't possibly know after kissing for a few hours only a few times in one year.

On the way home, I lose my thoughts in the lights streaming past me in a frenzied blur of whites and yellows along the highway, and I know that I am going to put more distance between us. Why can't he just leave things the way they are—easy, dreamlike, something I look forward to every couple of months? Why does he have to go and make protestations and offer cars that only reveal the banality of relationships? I don't want a fucking car. I want something else. I don't know what anymore. Just something. Something more. Something boundless and uninhabited by sex and obvious clichés. Just. More.

I think I find it when I come across Sean. Irish in appearance with blonde hair, blue eyes, and a short, stocky frame that lets me know he will only get bigger as he ages, I look past that. He's a lot like me. We frequent Malibu's each Saturday and dance together, and eventually, we end up kissing one night. The next Saturday, we kiss again. And the next Saturday after that. And the next until everyone in our circle knows to leave us alone whenever our bodies crash and move in rhythm on the dance floor for the next six months. We even go on a date. I take the Long Island Railroad to the Roslyn station where he picks me up and drives me to meet his mother and sisters, show me his room, and have lunch.

The chemistry is not existent between us during the day. I feel its absence. I am sure he does as well. Words are hard to find and when we do, they come out of our mouths like dry cotton balls that suck the saliva out of our mouths, leaving us gasping for hydration. When he kisses me at the station, it's a dry-mouthed one, not like the ones that drip with White Russian and beer at the club. We continue to meet at the clubs but don't go out again. We continue to kiss at the club and dance together until the club shuts down at four in the morning.

I like him so much that I buy him a card. A Hallmark card that tells him how connected I am to him, how much our trysts mean to me, and I take it with me to Malibu's one night, knowing he will be there. But as I enter the hall of the club, I see him, ten feet away from me, his lips attached to another girl, his arms bound to her shoulders, unaware of the audience of me and Joyce, who is as angry as I am, especially since she helped me find the right card that said enough without saying too much. The feelings I have for him wash away like grime rinsed off skin with soap and water, leaving me empty, wet, and alone. Again. I take the card, still in the envelope, sealed, with his name scribbled on the face of the envelope, and I tear it to shreds. I toss the fragments onto the floor and follow Joyce in the opposite direction—to the bar. Nothing a White Russian and some dancing can't fix.

When he sees me later that night, there is an edge to my smile, curtness to the words I manage to use in response to his questions. After a while, he gets the message and leaves. He calls me once or twice, and I am grateful for my machine, eating messages from boyish voices I have no intention of calling back, pressing the delete button until they disappear from my machine and my life with the irrevocable force of complete and utter silence.

After Sean, there are more of the ones I kiss on dance floors or by the bars and never see again, their faces hazy, indistinguishable images in a kaleidoscope, loose, fragmented eyes and noses and smiles that come and go with meaningless perpetuity.

And then there's Matt. Because Sean was not enough. The others were not enough to show me it is all fruitless, that I am chasing my tail like a stupid dog, that they are all the same, these boys.

Unlike the others, I find Matt in night school. We both take the same class for our education credentials, and I hear his voice addressing the professor from behind me before I see him. His voice is low and husky and it snakes into my hair, tugging at my head until I obey and turn around to find a pair of sea-blue orbs gazing back at me. He has shoulder-length blond hair that is pushed to the side of his face in waves, and I wonder what it will feel like to run my fingers through it. I turn my attention back to our professor, who is lecturing about fostering an inclusive learning environment in our classrooms through group work, but I am acutely aware of the blue set of eyes behind me, refusing to find him again, wondering why I hadn't seen him earlier, considering this is a month into the fall semester. It's because he spoke, and his words reveal an intelligence that I am attracted to rather than the dumb, vacant boys I have been finding on dizzying dance floors whose words don't matter as they circle around me set against the glaring music the DJ plays to numb us in liquor and sex.

I rush out of the class to catch the Q60 bus that will take me home. Night classes end at ten thirty, and if I don't get the bus, I will be waiting in front of Dunkin Donuts for at least forty minutes for the next one. And I hate waiting in front of the donut shop. The sweet and succulent scents of the donuts pull at me until my stomach groans in protest. I only have money for the bus. I don't have enough money for donuts. I'm broke. I'm still eating French fries from McDonald's that I make last the whole day, and this is enough until I get home. Then I rummage through my mother's refrigerator for food to eat. She doesn't cook for me, but the rule is that if I'm hungry, I can eat whatever is in there. So, I eat fruit. An apple. Watermelon in the summers, but then she gets mad because I only cut out the heart to eat, the sweet, juicy center, leaving the rest for her.

Most of the time, I am fine with not eating more than my French fries. I don't feel hungry, running from work to school to home and then back again. I am too busy to feel much of anything nowadays. I'm busy growing up, trying to be free. I look forward to the day when I finish my degree, find a full-time job, and then abandon the home that squeezes every bit of joy and youthfulness from me until there is nothing left but shapeless skin draped around fragments of dry and cracked bones. I hold on for life.

I meet the blue-eyed Germanic god the following week, before classes begin. I am at the cafeteria, paying in loose coins for a small cup of coffee that I need to get through the three-hour evening class. I find a seat and pull out my books to do some last-minute reading of the chapters our instructor assigned. Head buried in my pages, pen scratching notes in the margins, I stop short when I feel a presence beside me.

"Hey," he says, running his fingers through his thick waves and reshaping them to collect over his right ear.

"Hi," I reply, pen suspended in midair.

"We're in class together," he reminds me. "I'm Matt."

"Kathy," is all I can manage. He is tall, thin, and his blond goatee is perfectly trimmed above, below, and around his red lips. He is good-looking. He reminds me a lot of the Jesus Christ pictures I used to draw when I was little, wondering where he

204 & Marina DelVecchio

and God were when I needed them most. Matt is not Jesus Christ, but it's as if he has come alive from my imagination.

We sit next to each other in class, and he takes my number, asking if I'd like to go out with him sometime. I say, sure. Why not? Maybe he's different since he's not a guy I have met at the clubs. He's in graduate school. To be a teacher. Maybe this will be different. Let's see.

One night, we are on the phone.

"I have a confession to make to you," he offers.

"Oh yeah?"

"Yes. I can't date you. You see, I'm in love with someone else."

"Okay," I tell him, only a little bit disappointed. I mean, I just met him. Maybe we'll just be friends. I can use a guy friend. Both Chevy and Joe have faded into their own relationships, and I haven't seen them in a while. But it was nice having guy friends, going out with them and not feeling the pressure that comes with dating them. And Matt is a pretty guy, a pretty friend I find easy to talk to.

"So, is this your girlfriend?" I ask him out of curiosity.

"Not really. I mean, I've kissed her, but she's younger. She's still in high school, and I can't really have a relationship with her. She's also my boss's daughter, so that makes it so much more complicated. Do you think I'm nuts?"

"Nah," I laugh, "but it's pretty cliché. Falling in love with the boss's teenage daughter."

"I know," he sighs into the phone and I can see him running his fingers through his wavy hair. "I'm hopeless."

When we see each other the following week in class, he asks if I want to go out for dinner.

"As friends, though," I clarify.

He laughs, and the sound of it feels like cold refreshing water running over hot skin in the summertime.

"As friends," he agrees.

Sitting opposite each other in a local diner booth in Kew Gardens, we talk about God, philosophy, and education. He's smiling at me, and I find myself blushing beneath his unwavering gaze. He might as well be touching me. It would feel the same.

I tell him I'm an agnostic, and while I'm in the middle of my reasons, he leans over the tabletop and kisses me. It's a slow, steady kiss, just a lingering brush of lips on lips.

"Um, I thought you just wanted to be friends," I point out to him when he leans back into his seat again.

"I know. I'm sorry. I'm just sitting opposite you, and there's just something about you. You're so cute, I just had to kiss you."

"What about the girl you're so in love with?"

"That's just a juvenile infatuation, really." He changes the subject. "Don't you want to kiss me?"

I shrug my shoulders. "I could go either way. I was fine just being friends. I could use a male friend. Haven't had one in a while."

"I really like you. I like talking to you, being with you."

"I like talking to you, too." I smile weakly at him.

"And I really liked kissing just now. Would you be okay with me kissing you again?"

"So, kissing friends?"

"Yeah. Kissing friends." The smile he flashes me is crooked, sexy. "I think I'd like to kiss you again. Is that okay?"

"I prefer it if you kiss me without asking permission. Surprise me." I'm not always this good at flirting, but I think it helps that he's so beautiful, so earthy looking, so into me. He's easy to talk to. Easier to flirt with, to be sexy with. Who knows? Maybe this time I'm ready. For more. Maybe.

He doesn't kiss me just then. He waits, teasing me, surprising me, and I love it. I love the way he flirts, wanting so badly to grab a chunk of his thick blond hair and pull it towards me, press it to my cheek, wondering if it's as soft as it looks or coarse. But he keeps himself at bay, only grabbing my hand and interlocking our fingers as we walk out of the diner and to his car. When he drops me at my house, he gets out of his car, runs to my side, opens my door, and walks me to where my house stands. He's not the make-out-in-the-car kind of guy, and I find this refreshing, new. As I go to place the key into the lock, he takes my hand, turns me to face him, and then gently pushes me against the door. He's much taller than me, maybe five eleven to my five one, so I have to stand on my tippy toes, and he has to crouch down for us to kiss, and it's a nice kiss, one that fills the missing parts in me that all the other boys before him left open and gasping for relief. I enjoy the kiss, but I still arm myself against him. He has a crush on another girl, a young, pretty girl he's waiting to be of age. And we're just friends, kissing friends. I have to keep reminding myself of this.

At some point in our friendly-kissing-friendship, I end up falling for him. Maybe it's because he meets me in front of our class each week with a steaming cup of coffee, light on the milk and heavy on the sugar—just the way I like it. Maybe it's because he sits next to me in class and writes me notes, making me laugh and giggle when I should be learning about cooperative teaching and engaging students. It could be the way he looks at me right before he pulls me into his arms and kisses me, making me feel enveloped, swallowed by something big and wide, like a thick blanket of darkness hiding me from the rest of the world, allowing me to give in, sink into the firm arms and chest that cradle me. Or it could be the way we argue about literature—half-laughing, or that he gives me a copy of *Voltaire* for Christmas, signing the inside with his name, addressing it to me, his lovely friend and kissing buddy. It's the first gift I've received by a boy, and the fact that it's a classic that we have discussed and analyzed in our heated discussions holds meaning in my small, aching heart. Or maybe it's that he challenges me.

"You know," he begins one day as we talk on the phone at two in the morning, "you always expect me to pick you up, take you somewhere, pick where we go, and so on. I do for you, but you don't do much in return."

"What do you want me to do?"

"I don't know. Something. I feel like I give more than you." There is a pause. "Like maybe you can surprise me at work one day—the way I surprise you. You can bring me dinner for once. I come to your job all the time. You have to give a little bit."

I am surprised at this. He wants me to give, but he's not asking for sex or more heavy petting. He's asking for a surprise visit at work. A slice of pizza. He's right. I don't think about guys. What they want. I have learned to discredit their needs since their needs seem to revolve around sex. But Matt is not asking for that. He's asking for consideration. To be thought of, for me to be thoughtful of him, to show him that I care about him.

So, the next time he's at work, I do just that. I trek into Manhattan one evening when I know he will be in the office. He works at a music production company, and when I arrive, with two slices of pizza and a Coke for him, we are alone. He works the night shift, closing past midnight. He smiles when he opens the door to find me, and it warms me, knowing that this is all I have to do to please him. He shows me around the small office he works in, and then we end up on the floor, kissing. He takes off my glasses, which I always keep on my face, a shield between me and the rest of the world. I close my eyes so he can't see into me.

"Open your eyes," he coaxes. "I won't kiss you until you do."

I sigh aloud, my breath forcing long blond hair to move above me, tickling my nose. But I open them, averting them from the piercing shades of blue that want to peer into me longer and deeper than I prefer. I feel his lips on mine, his hands moving my face so that my eyes meet his when he pulls away from me slightly, and then his gaze nestles into mine, and it's like we're making love, talking to each other without words.

"I am so mesmerized by you," he whispers before kissing me again. It's all so moving, I want to cry. A low, deep wail that comes when you feel seen and loved. Open. And loved, anyway.

"Can I read you something?" he asks me an hour later, listening to music from the booth he manages with skillful hands pushing and pulling knobs that have no labels anywhere in sight.

"Uh huh," I mumble.

And then he reads me this poem, this lovely, passionate poem about taking the virginity of a young girl with blond hair and green eyes that overtake him like a thick forest of leafy trees. He notes the blood, evidence of her innocence dying in his arms, taking it in the palm of his hands like a sacred gem, her girlishness transformed into womanhood, her legs wrapping around him like vines he surrenders to.

My bones grow cold, and I wonder why he wants to read this to me. Me. The girl he's kissing while desiring someone else. Someone he can't have. I rush out of the booth, run down the stairs, and walk to the train station—all without saying a word to him. When he calls for me, I keep walking, keep moving away from the warmth of his kisses and touches and words that belie his heart, his own yearnings. Yearnings that have nothing to do with me. Kissing buddy indeed. That is all that I am. But he told me from the start. He loved someone else, someone not old enough to date, so why are there stupid tears streaming down my face in the middle of the train station, in front of strangers, in the middle of the night?

I am alone. I feel nothing. That's not true. I feel pain, an ache that shatters bones into fragmented slivers catapulted all around me. I am sinking into myself, like quicksand, with nothing to hold onto, to pull me out, to press air into my lungs.

And then I make a decision. When the tears cool and the cold winter air freezes them onto my skin, I decide to take a break. From dating. From kissing. No more. I will not date anyone, no matter how cute he is, how sweetly his eyes flirt with mine. I am done.

So, when Matt calls me a few days later, I am no longer the girl he knows. I am distant, cold, responding to him in monosyllabic stupor.

"Why are you being so belligerent?" he asks after a while.

"I'm not," is my curt response. I am not there. I am far away. Too far for him to find me. The girl he only wants as a kissing buddy.

"Do you even know what the word means?" His voice is harsh and his words invite a sardonic grin on my face that he can't see. I take the opening he gives me.

"It means fuck you." I hang up. I end it. End us. Just like that. Like it's nothing.

VIRGIN, PLAIN AND SIMPLE

For the next month or so, my life is simple. Plain. Quiet. Lonely, sure. But it's better than the expectations that come with dating. Expectations boys have for sex. Expectations I have for something more, like they're going to be different. Like this one is actually going to be the one, the one who will change everything.

I throw myself into work and school, and now that the new semester has begun, Matt is no longer in my class. I see him on campus here and there, his eyes following me, but I pretend he's not there. He does not exist. Not for me.

I am at work one morning, having snuck into the side door, late again. I have a hard time waking up on time. I am tired. All the time. My muscles are heavy and pull me down, as if I have anchors attached to my ankles and wrists. Moving is cumbersome, and I throw myself into the shower every morning just to find the energy to pull myself together, but it doesn't work. I lumber my way through each day, from job to job, and then from school to the dark room that lulls me into a deep sleep and tugs at my waist, my legs, when my alarm rings and I fight to get out of bed.

My supervisor, the lead librarian at Rego Park Library, asks me into her office. I move from the children's section of books to her office as if the floor is made up of mud, raising my knees high, just to get the traction I need to be mobile, forward-moving. Mrs. Jenkins points to the leather chair opposite her, in front of her chestnut lacquered desk, and I sink into it as if it's a body of water about to fill my lungs.

"I know I was late today. I'm sorry. I'll try to wake up earlier," I begin. When she continues to sit across from me still and quiet, I add, "I walk here and sometimes I underestimate how long it takes to arrive on time."

She waves her hand to the right and shakes her head at me.

"Kathy, you're a hard worker. You've been working here since you were sixteen. You can be late once in a while. That's not why I called you here."

I am relieved. "Okay." I wait for her to explain.

She rises from her leather chair and moves to the window, looking out at the sun and traffic and bustle of people strolling past the small building I have made my second home all these years, fostering in me love of books and stories and words I find difficult to utter with my small voice.

"Your mother called here the other day." She pauses, looking at me, as if trying to gauge my response.

I am mute. The mention of my mother has that kind of effect on me. What now?

She continues. "She asked me to decrease the hours you work during the week. She says you're tired all the time and working too much."

I panic, my pulse racing with such speed beneath my skin I wonder if she can see it.

"What did you tell her?" I ask, my voice raspy, breathless in the way that it gets whenever I am confronted with anger. "I need this job," I tell her. "I'm working two jobs to pay for graduate school. I can't decrease my hours." I'm furious at my mother. Why does she always have to get in the way? Calling my friends and boyfriends is one thing. I can ignore that because it lets me know who is loyal to me, who stands up for me. But my boss? Interfering with my job, the money I need to pay for school? This is another thing altogether.

"I told her to mind her own business," Mrs. Jenkins's stern response cuts into my thoughts.

I almost smile. I sigh with relief. "What did she say?" No one stands up to my mother like this. At least, I've never witnessed it. I would like to see it, experience it for myself. Just once.

"She hung up on me. The truth is, this is your job and if you want fewer hours, that is up to you. But you don't sound like you do."

"No. In fact, I wish I could work here full time."

"Unfortunately, the only full-time positions we have is for librarians. You're in grad school for teaching, right?"

"Yes," I nod. "I want to teach literature to high school students."

She sits back in her chair opposite me and runs her gaze over me. "You know, you're a pretty girl. You should fix your hair, wear some makeup. Put a little effort into your appearance. You might feel a little better about yourself."

At this, I clamp my mouth shut. *You don't know me*, I want to snap at her, but politeness keeps me silent. Always polite. Meanwhile, people around me say whatever they want. Whenever they want. Like her. Now. "Is that all?" I ask, moving out of my chair and glancing towards the door through which I would like to escape.

"Yes. That's all." She assumes a more professional tone.

"Thanks for your time," I tell her. I want my job, so respect reigns. But as soon as I exit her office, I know I have to look for another job.

My friend Jody comes to the rescue. She is one of my middle school friends who found me while I was still working in the mall.

Married at twenty-one, she works for a pharmaceutical company in Whitestone and offers to get me an interview with her supervisor. I want this job. All I have to do is file reports and after a five-minute interview, I am offered a job that will pay me ten dollars an hour for as many hours as I want to work during the week. This means I can quit both my jobs—the one at the library with the nosy librarian and the one at the rental company where men slap my ass and write offensive letters of recommendation that speak of my sex as if it's a commodity. When I tell Steve I'm quitting, he wants to have a longer conversation in the conference room—just the two of us—to make it professional and official.

After I explain to him that I found one job that will pay me more and not limit my hours instead of working two jobs to pay for school, he tells me he understands and shakes my hand. I don't tell him that although the owner of the place is a man, I will be working in an office with six women and the chances of them harassing me is non-existent. I don't tell him that the dress code for women is sexist, or that the sexual innuendo and sexist behavior of the men in the office is inexcusable, unconstitutional. I think it. All of it. But I don't say it. Because I am too polite, too nice, too timid to make myself be heard by a man twenty years my senior.

Then he drops his pencil. I bend down to pick it up for him.

"While you're down there," he laughs. "I'm kidding. Just kidding."

I'm glad to be leaving. Is this what men are like at work, away from their wives and kids? I mean, Steve is your run-of-the-mill kind of guy. He's ordinary, and aside from this sexist shit, he appears to be a good guy. *I hope he has a daughter one day*, I think as I recall the pictures on his desk showcasing the happy smiles of his wife and two little boys. I am somebody's daughter. I am somebody.

"Do me a favor," he adds as I move towards the door of the conference room. "Don't go around telling the other girls you're making more money at this new job. It's not professional, okay?" He tosses me a careless smile that does not acknowledge his own unprofessional behavior.

"Sure," I smile back.

I hook up three girls with interviews once I am settled in my new job as a file clerk. They are three of Steve's best workers and my new boss hires them.

Fuck him.

A VIRGIN'S FIRST BET

"That's not fair," quips a deep, throaty voice loud enough to be heard over the blaring clamor of rock music thrashing against the walls of the bar.

Shirley and I stand a few feet away from the stage at the Crazy Moose Saloon, a bar we frequent every Thursday night on Bell Boulevard, after our beloved episodes of *90210* and *Melrose Place* finish. They have a live band that plays our favorite songs, and as we nurse our drinks, we sing along with the lead guitarist and sway our hips to the rhythm.

The music has died down and girls of various sizes, shapes, and hair color are making their way onto the stage. At the age of twenty-four and in graduate school, Shirley and I feel much older and more mature than the girls vying for the "Sexiest Girl" contest about to take place on the stage before us.

We roll our eyes at each other and laugh at the spectacle these young women are about to make of themselves. Some nights, just for fun, Shirley and I go to strip clubs and picket outside their doors, screaming for the sex-starved men on the buses that bring them in herds to run back into its secure enclosure and be driven to another one—one that doesn't have girls like us to remind them they are exploiting women who don't look like their wives and daughters. On this night, however, we are celebrating Shirley's engagement, so we stick it out.

"That's so unfair," the booming voice calls out again. He is standing beside me now. "This is so sexist. Why do only girls get to compete for the title? They should have a contest for us, too."

"Go on, go up there," I yell over the music without looking at him. "I'll vote for you."

I give him a sideways glance, but not long enough to make out what he looks like. I think he's funny, and I love that a guy finds this contest as ridiculous as we do. But I'm not interested in meeting anyone or in hooking up. Matt is still a bitter note on my tongue, and I have no desire to revisit love and its transient spells that leave me cold and broken.

"I think I know him," Shirley whispers in my ear.

"Oh, yeah?"

"Yeah. I think he went to Prep."

"So ask him."

"Nah," she shakes her head, her wavy blond hair swishing between us. "It doesn't matter, anyway."

"Hey," I suddenly turn to the funny guy still lingering beside me, stealing glimpses at me. My White Russian in one hand, I loosen Shirley's fingers from my arm with the other, letting out a squeal when she pinches my sides. "My friend thinks she knows you. Did you go to Prep?"

"Yeah," he responds. He and his friend approach our circle of two.

He and Shirley take a closer look at each other and then it finally registers that they had hung out and smoked together at a park during his senior and her junior year at St. Francis Prep.

"I'm Joe," he says, his smile is big and toothy. Because Shirley knows him, I loosen my grip over my limbs and warm up to him.

"Why aren't you up there?" he asks me, pointing to the row

of ten girls standing by the edge of the platform before us. In the background, the MC is asking the girls a series of questions and then inviting them to dance for the crowd. Boisterous beer-guzzling guys crowd around us to get closer to the girls on stage and cheer for their choices.

"Me?" I laugh. "That's not my scene."

I could say more. I often do, but people get wary when they find themselves on the receiving end of my impassioned feminist speeches about girls voluntarily subjecting themselves to sexism and social otherness. Most people in their twenties just want to have fun, not analyze the impact their actions have on the female gender. I have come to recognize their disinterest in the way their eyes seem to grow tired and hazy, seeking something better, lighter, over my shoulder.

"So, who do you think will win the contest?" he inquires.

"Oh, probably the blond one with the revealing breasts. Look at her—all the guys are drooling."

"You think she's the sexiest out of all of them?" he gives me an incredulous look.

"Of course. Even I think she's hot. You don't?" I return his look with a you-gotta-be-kidding-me one.

"No. Not at all. I think she's trying too hard to be sexy. But she isn't."

At this point, I turn to face him and get a close look at the only guy in the room who is not experiencing a physical response to the luscious blond parading her curves in stripper-like movements for the thrill of masculine whistles and cheers.

He has reddish dark brown hair that is combed back and sprayed to perfection, so as not to move. Although his hand gestures and thick New York accent scream Italian, the pink hue of his skin and hazel eyes reveal the presence of Irish ancestry. The color of his eyes changes when the lights shift above us to the beat of the music the girls are shaking their ample hips to, and I find myself unraveling the varying hues of green and blue and gray threads that reveal themselves when his long lashes pull open the lids of his eyes—soft, electric eyes that invite me to join the fun flitting and shimmying in them.

He is thin and tall, and I like the way his short-sleeved shirt is pulled tightly across the expanse of his chest and the protruding bulge of his biceps. He isn't massively built, but his physical strength is obvious and fits perfectly with his thin frame.

I find myself inching closer toward him to smell the musky scent of his cologne. I like the way he looks at me, his eyes peering down at me from his five-nine frame, half-hooded by the blond-reddish lashes threatening to conceal the multi-colored layers of his eyes from me.

There is a silent, invisible chemistry pulsing between us, and the more time we spend talking, joking, flirting, the stronger it becomes, drawing our bodies closer, our heads bending towards each other, cheek to cheek, just so we can hear the other's voice in our ear.

"Okay," I tell him placing my hand on the curve of my hip and cocking my head to the side. "If the blond one isn't sexy in your eyes, then which one of those girls do you think will win the contest?"

He withdraws his glance from me and scans the remaining three girls who have won the crowd's approval. "That one over there, at the end."

"The plain one?" I give him a look of skepticism. "The one with the short brown hair and minimal makeup?"

"Yeah."

"How do you figure that?"

"She's sexy without trying. She's not showing off her chest or any skin. She's just out there having fun. She's not playing to the crowd or pretending to be more than she is. She's confident without being aggressive with her sexuality. Even her dance is sexy. It's not over the top. That is sexy. That's what's going to make her win."

"Over the blond one?"

"The blond one is over the top. Slutty is not sexy."

I say nothing. I'm impressed by his candor. Moreover, I am impressed with the easy rapport we have between us. I don't usually talk to guys like this, except my guy friends. At some point in the evening, I seem to have shed my protective veneer, my shyness, and I have begun to be myself, the way I am only with my friends, saying whatever I feel like saying. Or saying nothing. Even silence sits comfortably between us, and it's easy, talking to him. Maybe it's because I am not thinking about hooking up. I'm not thinking about kissing him or dating him. I'm just being.

"Let's make a bet," he breaks into my thoughts.

"Okay," I laugh. "What are the conditions?"

"If I win, you buy me a drink. If you win, I buy you a drink."

I smile. Either way, we both win.

Of course, I lose the bet, and I stand there impressed that the sweet, low-key brunette with brown eyes, clad in jeans and T-shirt, wins the sexiest girl contest over the sultry blond with boundless breasts—although she loses points for being in the contest in the first place—but whatever. I buy Joe his Budweiser and he lets me. The way he's looking at me makes me feel as if this is part of a test, and I'm passing because I don't renege on the bet or try to make him buy my drink.

Two hours, two beers, and one White Russian later, we are still standing by the bar, talking, laughing, joking. Time subtracts the space that separates us. Every time we laugh or need to hear what the other says, we inch closer to one another, closing any remaining space between us. His breath fans my cheek when he speaks to me, and I am drowsy with want. I want to kiss him, to feel myself wrapped inside his warmth, feel as beautiful and desired as his eyes tell me I am.

I let him touch me.

At some point, his left hand finds its way to my waist, and for the past half hour, he has been caressing the green velvet fabric of my shirt—my onesie.

"So," he whispers in my ear, dulling my senses.

I want to lean the back of my head onto the bar and offer my body to his hands. "Discover me, free me," I want to tell him. But I remain quiet, reveling in the heat growing in my belly and rising to my chest. I have felt this before. With many guys since John—the college John who first broke me—using their mouths and arms to make me forget him—but I have never wanted to explore the uncharted territory of my desires. I have always kept them in check, the same way my mother keeps me in check, shutting down, closing down, pushing their hands and mouths away from me without a moan of regret or difficulty.

"I'm immune to you," I tell them coldly when they ask how I can shut down so completely, so quickly. "Like a water faucet," my old John used to complain.

This is different. Joe is different. My whole body trusts his touch. I trust him. And this is a strange thing to say, coming from me, from someone who has lost the ability to trust and love openly—and let's not forget—has sworn off guys since the Matt debacle.

"So," he says again. "Where do you want to go for our first date?"

"I don't know." I want to tell him that I am not dating for a while, for long enough to regain my strength, figure out what I want, but I don't say any of this. I feel ready. I feel strong.

"Well," he prods, "what are your usual dates like?"

"Oh, you know, movie and dinner, not especially in that order. What about you?"

"Same. That's so boring, don't you think?"

I shrug my shoulders. I love going to the movies. Like books, they help me escape life for at least two hours. "What do you suggest then?"

"How about the zoo?" he recommends after a moment's hesitation.

"The zoo," I repeat, nodding my head in approval. "That sounds great. I don't think I've ever been to the zoo for a first date, or any date for that matter."

"You like it?"

"Yeah, I do. What made you think of it?"

"I just took my nephew last weekend. He's three years old, and we had a great time. I just thought it'd be something different than the usual boring stuff we do on dates. It would set our date apart, don't you think?"

"Uh huh." I tilt my head and give him a suspicious look. "Do you take all your dates there, to impress them?"

"Actually, most girls aren't impressed by the zoo for a first date. They'd rather have dinner at a nice restaurant."

"Really? I'd rather have the zoo."

"Why?"

"There are less pretensions at the zoo. You can be yourself and not worry about wearing a fancy dress, ordering fancy food, or having polite conversation. We can get to know each other better, easier, at the zoo, and not care about making the right impression. You know what I mean?"

"Yes, I do."

He caresses the fabric of my shirt again, below my rib cage. I suck in my breath, mesmerized by his touch, by the look he is giving me just now. I have the strongest urge to giggle, to grab his hand and place it on my breast, to throw myself into his arms and kiss him.

I do nothing.

I only watch. I watch him watch me.

"May I kiss you?" His voice is low and so close to my face that all I have to do is open my lips to receive him.

"Yes." I want to kiss him, too, despite my promise to give up boys and dating.

But as he leans forward, his lips centimeters from my own, I chicken out and turn my head. His lips, soft, tender, caress the skin of my cheek.

"I really want to kiss you," he confesses to me, his face still close to mine.

"I do, too, but we have time. Like you said, I just want this to be different. I could kiss you like I kiss every other guy I meet at bars, but why ruin it? Why make this a common thing, when it hasn't been so far?"

I hope he isn't turned off by this idea, or playing with me, but if he is, then I have lost nothing. I can still keep my promise to myself. If I'm going to play this game, then I am going to play it differently. My way.

To kiss him at the bar will make him just like every other guy I have kissed an hour, half an hour after I meet him. They mean nothing, the guys or the kisses. They have given me pleasure, momentary flight from the bitter toward the sweet and decadent, but they have not lasted, have never meant anything more. They have been easy to walk away from, to replace with another face, another set of hands, another pleasing mouth in which to find my solace.

"I'll call you tomorrow," he tells my ear when Shirley comes over to see if I'm ready to leave. He kisses my cheek, and I feel his eyes on me as we exit the bar.

It is February. A New York kind of February, frigid, with mean, hard-hitting winds, but my insides are flushed with heat and an odd surge of longing.

A VIRGIN'S AWAKENING

Joe calls me the next evening, just as he has promised. He doesn't play games. He doesn't say he will call and then wait three days to do so. He calls the next day, and we talk on the phone until three in the morning, telling each other everything we want the other to know. We make plans to go out the next day, Saturday, to the zoo. But with Saturday morning comes a blizzard, and Queens looks like a white desert, cars and streets covered with sheets of pure, untouched snow ploughs and footsteps have yet to disturb. It is quiet, still, the ugly noises and chaos of city life buried, sleeping, awakened only by force.

"We can still go to the zoo," Joe tells me over the phone. "We'll just meet there. Take the train."

But I'm too tired to go out. Too lazy to move. I hate the cold. I want to stay indoors, in my bed, and not even Joe can make me change my mind. So we agree on a midday Monday date instead.

Of course, the day creeps in disastrously. After the weekend snowstorm, our pipes freeze, and I'm unable to take a shower. I never begin the day without a shower. It's how I wake up, feeling fresh and clean and armed to face the day. I am tempted to call Joe and cancel our date, but since I canceled the date to the zoo that Saturday, I know if I cancel this one, he will not ask me for another.

I wake up irritated that I can't wash the sleep out of my eyes. I apply concealer on my face, makeup I don't usually wear, to hide the blue shadows beneath my eyes. I line my lips with dark brown lipstick I don't leave the house without first applying. I dress in my usual jeans, crotch-snapping shirt, and a plaid shirt, finishing off the ensemble with my timberland boots.

There is not much I can do with my stringy light brown hair. By midday, it will look greasy and drab, but with all the water frozen in our pipes, there is nothing I can do to fix it. I push the fine, shoulder-length strands behind my ears and straighten my bangs with my fingertips, pulling them down to meet my eyes. Casting a disgruntled look at my appearance in the mirror, I dismiss myself and run down the stairs and out to the garage to wait for the plumber who will thaw out our pipes.

An hour later, Joe arrives in his sister's car to pick me up. He doesn't have his own car. Up until a year ago, he rode a motorcycle, which was destroyed in a crash that left him with a broken coccyx bone and some scrapes and bruises on his back, arms, and legs.

I am very awkward around him. Uncomfortable, really. Self-conscious. Not only do I not look or feel my best for our first date, but it is also the first time I am seeing him since the first night we met. Although we didn't kiss, the sexual energy between us had swarmed around us like a collective mob of bees on the hunt for honey. We reacted to that sexual energy comfortably, the dimly lit bar and alcohol embracing our desires without exposing any flaws or the natural hues of reality. I keep thinking about his fingers tracing the velour fabric of my shirt and wonder what he will want to get away with during the day, when it is not dark or loud or seductive.

I keep my gaze averted from Joe's, sure that I will find his eyes focusing on the blotchiness of my skin or the pimples that have so generously decided to visit me on this one day I cannot shower. I am more comfortable with myself at night. She flatters me with her gentle moonlit hues and cloaks me with a veneer of confidence that day only manages to strip me of, making me feel exposed and naked.

"Do you want to come inside?" I offer, shyly glancing up at him. He looks just as good in the day as he had Thursday evening. His pipes haven't frozen.

"Sure."

I am quietly put at ease by his smile. It is wide, genuine, its warmth cascading over me, filling me with a sweet thrill I have sworn not to feed into again.

Joe is only the third boy I have let into my mother's home without her present. Danny had been my first. At the cusp of twenty-four, I am still forbidden to let anyone inside my mother's home. With the exception of the old John, none of my friends or dates have seen the inside of the cell I inhabit. And aside from seeing her head sticking out of the window when they come to pick me up, no one has met my mother face-to-face.

This is how she likes it, wants it. Her matriarch head peering down at the subjects of her revulsion, her small, cold, dark eyes following them down the block until they are miniscule black spots she can wipe out with the closing of her window. She is a formidable woman, and many fear her. Even me.

I don't know why I lead Joe past the forbidding threshold, up the stairs, and into my mother's austere den. Everything else has been so different between us, why not this? Why not let him into the side of myself no one ever sees? I want to break patterns,

patterns that leave me heart-broken and unhappy. I want him to see it, see me, see the mess of my life . . . and I want to see if he runs.

He doesn't. He retraces my steps and follows me into my unspoken grief with a quiet confidence and strength that consoles the wounds buried in my chest.

Joe's presence warms the cold, bitter interior of the home I have grown up in without love or affection, and somewhere deep inside me, I feel that this is the right thing, that he is the right person, that this is the right time.

I feel no shame or guilt.

And when I show him my room, I concentrate on his reaction as if he is a specimen under a microscope.

His eyes widen when he catches a glimpse, and a quick whiff, of the chaos I inhabit. As usual, my room is in utter disarray. The bed is unmade, my clothes are scattered all over the floor, and a pile of plates and utensils crowd the top of my dresser. Since I eat in my room and am too lazy to clean up after myself, maggots grow and squirm in the leftover food, forcing me to run the dishes into the kitchen and under hot water until the maggots burn and drown to their deaths; and let's not even bring up the cat litter box that has not been cleaned in days, infusing my room with a malodorous stench that not even opened windows can dispel and forcing Treasure, my tabby, to do her new business on top of old business.

He looks at me and sees more than I can offer him with words. I look away from his probing look, hoping he isn't disgusted by the state of my existence. I close the door to my room and draw him towards my mother's room. It is as opposite as our natures, clinically neat and formal.

He does not enter the room. He only stands in the hall and looks into it.

As I exit my mother's room, I stumble and gently bump into him. We hardly touch, but our eyes meet and something about the moment robs me of my breath. I feel a surge of electricity pass through my body, and it is unlike anything I have ever experienced before. I wonder if he feels it as well but dare not ask. Flustered, I lead him into the other rooms, and finally, down the stairs and out of my home. I breathe for the first time when the wintry, unyielding air hits my face and stings my eyes, making them tear.

We have arranged a typical date, movies and lunch, because I have a graduate class in the evening. But everything about it touches a unique nerve in my body, the parts of me that have been deserted and overlooked.

"I thought," he says, "that we'd see that movie *Before Sunrise*, about a couple that spends the day together on a tour in Europe. They have a day date, like us, and they fall in love. Ethan Hawke is in it. You said you liked him, right?"

"Yeah, he's one of my favorites." I turn my head away from him to hide the pleasure I feel. I have felt this reeling sensation before, with other guys, but I never tire of the wonder that comes with the newness of a relationship. I just don't want him to be like the others. I don't want to be disappointed again.

Walking beside him to the car, I realize that I love first everythings. There is nothing that can compare with the wild array of stirrings accompanying first glances, dates, kisses, touches . . . anything that happens for the first time affords a moment of awe. But time and change smash into it like a car pile-up, leaving transitory scars in their wake. Experience drains the novelty through a sieve that collects memories but not moments. Newness is drained, leaving behind nothing but a fleeting recollection of what is lost and irretrievable.

This is how it has always been, and even as I sit beside Joe on our first date, anticipating our first kiss, our first touch, I'm afraid it won't last. Nothing ever does. Nothing ever has. I want to prolong each moment I spend with him, taste every second, every word he utters in my favor, before it all sifts through my fingers like loose grains of sand separated from its earthy origins.

I think of my mother. She is never far from my mind. Hers is the prevailing voice in my head. Her harsh words and bitterness accompany me everywhere.

She loved me once, the newness of me, when she had first met me in Greece and adopted me. She raved about how sweet and smart I was then, but when I no longer resembled that child, her perception of that child, she lost interest in me. I wonder how it is that I have become so much like her. Do we always end up resembling those we live with, our personalities meshing until there are no discernible differences between us?

My thoughts return to the winds that have brought me here, to this spot, standing in front of Joe. Good, funny, down-to-earth Joe, loose snowflakes flitting through the icy air between us and landing in our hair.

"Look," he points to a stairway adjacent to the movie theatre. "We have time before the movie begins. Do you want to go check out the art gallery?"

"I love art galleries," I beam at him, forgetting for a moment my greasy, unwashed face and hair.

"Are you an artist?" he asks.

I laugh. "No way. I can't even draw a straight line, but I love looking at the world through artists' eyes, the way they see it."

As we browse through the artwork displayed in the gallery, Joe touches my hand to show me a painting he likes. He doesn't let go. He holds onto my hand the entire date.

After the movie, we go to Pizzeria Uno's on Bell Boulevard for lunch.

"I live around here, you know," he tells me over pizza and Coke.

"Yeah, you told me the night we met. On 42nd, right?"

"Good memory. I'd show you my apartment, but your class starts soon."

"I can be a little late. I'd love to see where you live."

"Maybe some other time. On our next date. Anyway, Tasha will get upset if I go home and then leave immediately after."

"Who's Tasha?"

"She's my baby," he smiles. "She's a full-haired Akita, a great bear of a dog. She'll poo all over the apartment if we go over there for just a few minutes and then leave."

"Oh, I love dogs. I'd love to meet her."

"What about Saturday? Maybe we can spend the day together, go to the zoo."

"I can't on Saturday. Shirley and I are big buddies and we're spending the day with our kids."

"Kids?"

"Yeah, they live in homeless shelters. My girl's name this year is Nakya and she's only nine. Every weekend, Shirley and I take our girls out, usually to the city. We go to museums and the library, and wherever else we can think of to take them."

"How did you get into that?"

"Through school."

"You know, a lot of people our age wouldn't even bother with that kind of . . . social service. Why do you do it?"

"It gives me something to do other than obsess about my problems."

"That's very nice of you," he says, taking a sip from his cream soda. "I couldn't do it. I give you a lot of credit."

I don't know what it is about him, but I want to tell him. So, I do. "I was homeless. A long time ago. Before I was adopted." I can see the words contained in small bubbles floating in the spaces between us, singular, fragile, about to burst. My heart beats loudly in my chest. I can feel it hammering against my insides, in my ears. It's almost deafening.

He doesn't say anything, as if he knows I've never told a soul before. That these are virgin words. That he's the first to receive them. And he waits, holding his breath, ready to cup them in his hands and nurture them like rare gems that have never seen the light before.

"My dad left us. My mother couldn't afford our home, so we lost it and lived on the streets for a while. For a year. So, when I saw the flyer, I just felt like it was pulling me. It was a way to connect with that part of myself."

"That's tough," he says, his fingers finding mine atop the table.

His touch brings me back to the present, to the raw nerves I have exposed, and I quickly withdraw my fingers and smile an apology for the abrupt shift in mood. "And I also get three credits and an A to boost my GPA," I add with a nervous laugh.

He takes the hint and shifts with me. "You mean you don't have a straight 4.0 average? I thought you were a brain."

I laugh aloud. "I am. But I had a really bad semester and my grades plummeted. The Big Buddy Program helped me get back to where I needed to be, and because of it, I was able to make up that bad semester and realize that teaching is what I want to do with my life."

"What happened to make your grades plummet?" Joe asks, taking a bite from his pizza.

"It's kind of embarrassing, really." I offer a sheepish grin.

"What?"

"I had my heart broken." I'm surprised at my own honesty. I don't speak to anyone about John. I've never said these words aloud before, not even to my girlfriends. What is this power Joe has to make me feel this open, this honest? This safe.

"Really?"

"Yeah. He was my first real boyfriend, and he dumped me for another woman, an older one. I spent the entire semester hanging out at the student union where he worked, just to prove to him that he didn't hurt me. Of course, I hurt myself. In more ways than one."

"Why did he break up with you?"

I look at him and release a heavy sigh, as if I am lifting a 50-pound weight off my chest. "I wouldn't sleep with him."

"Why wouldn't you sleep with him?"

"I wasn't ready. Having sex is a big thing for me, and I just couldn't."

"Did you love him?"

"I guess not enough to have him be the first."

WARNING: VIRGIN DEAD AHEAD!!! I can see the lights flashing in his head.

Joe gives me a thoughtful look. "Are you a virgin?"

"Yeah. Am I scaring you away, yet?"

"Why would I be scared? I think it's great. You don't find too many twenty-four-year-old virgins out there today."

"I'm glad that's out of the way," I let out a short, forced laugh.

"Why?"

"I just think it's better that we start off knowing where the other stands, that's all."

"So, you're warning me?"

"No . . . preparing you more like it. I'm very proud of who I am, and it's not something I'm going to give up after four months or even six months. Only when I'm ready." I arm myself, feeling hot all over.

His eyes survey me lightly. "You've given this speech before." It isn't a question.

I shrug my shoulders.

"Listen," he leans closer to me and takes hold of my hand on the table.

He hesitates, and I watch as he examines my fingers. I know what he is frowning at. The nail beds on all my fingers resemble the length and frailty of an infant's fingernails. I have been biting my nails since I was a child. They never grew beyond the skin of my fingertips. I don't let them. I chew on them, and when there are no more nails left, I chew on the skin around them. I don't stop until my fingers are raw, red, and beginning to ache.

I pull my hands away from his, from his probing eyes, and pretend to need them in order to take a sip from my Coke.

"Kath," he begins again. "Let's make a deal. When sex becomes an issue for us, then we'll talk about it. Okay? You don't need to warn me or prepare me. Right now, I'm just happy to get to know you. I like being with you. Okay?"

"Okay," I say, smiling.

As I sit opposite Joe, I feel the urge to put my whole life on the table for him to see. I have this feeling that he will understand all my pain—not just with fleeting love but also with my mother and the way she degrades me. I have never felt this way before. He is so deep and open and intuitive that I know he sees more than any other guy has seen in me. He sees into my words as if they are images that I paint for him, and this forces me to see him past the simple stereotype of guys that I have created for myself to stay sane and safe. Or maybe he wants to see more— more than just a girl to fuck.

He's not like any guy I have ever dated before, and the knowledge of this leaves me breathless, expectant, curious.

"You know," he begins, lowering his head in search of my eyes, which I try to conceal behind my glasses. "I'm not ready to end our date."

I raise my eyes to find his. I smile. "I'm having a good time, too."

"What time do you get out of school tonight?"

"Around eight. But I have to make a trip to the bookstore and buy my books for the term. Why?"

"I was just thinking. Maybe I can pick you up after your class. We can grab a late dinner."

"You sure?"

"Yeah," he laughs. "I'm having a really good time. I don't want it to end."

"Okay," I say, nodding.

"Yeah?"

"Yeah." We both look at each other and start laughing.

Joe drives me to school, and two and a half hours later picks me up for the second part of our date.

We go to a diner on Queens Boulevard where he has a grilled cheese sandwich and I have cheesecake and cappuccino. I'm not a big eater. The only time I eat is at work and only because everyone else is eating, often asking me for my order. I always get a salad with chicken and mozzarella balls covered in blue cheese. It's the same thing every day and the only meal I have each day. If I'm not working, chances are I won't eat anything that day.

The day I meet Joe, I begin to eat. He makes sure of it.

He gives me a piggyback ride into the diner and, wanting to prove that I am his equal in strength, I give him one, a short one, out to his car, when we leave. He lets me, noting how important it is to me that I carry my own weight, that I pay for my own way, that I am just as strong as he is.

"So," he leans toward me after parking his car in front of my mother's driveway. "I'll call you tomorrow. Maybe we can still make it to the zoo one of these days."

"Okay," is all I can muster. My head is fuzzy with the want of his kiss. I turn my face to him and grin. His lips gently touch the corner of mine, and I am disappointed that he doesn't try to kiss me deeper, longer.

I would have let him.

I let myself inside my mother's three-story apartment building and trudge up the stairs with a collection of fragmented emotions charging against my insides.

I fall asleep that night with the realization that there is more. There is more out there, more than this. There is more inside me, more to me, more than this.

I turn and twist into my sheets wanting more more than anything.

A VIRGIN'S CHEATING HEART

I want to say that I am good with Joe. That I am loyal. But then I would be a liar. I am too scared to be good, to be honest, to be loyal to the boy who takes me to school each night and then picks me up so I don't have to take a bus, takes me to the local diner to buy me dinner because I don't eat—even when he doesn't have enough money to pay his rent. For the next six months, he treats me like I am somebody. Somebody special. Somebody worthy of time, affection, love even. But I'm so jaded, I don't believe any of it. That all of this can be real. Or maybe I do, and this is why I try so hard to sabotage us—what could result in us—if I let it.

While I see him before and after work and school, I don't see him on the nights I go out with my friends. Every Thursday, Friday, and Saturday night still goes to me, to my friends, to my White Russians, to our dancing in a small circle, alcohol swiveling inside us, guys whirling outside of us like vultures on the hunt for blood, for easy carcasses stumbling into dark corners too inebriated to see or speak or say no.

I still kiss guys. Not a lot of them. Not like I used to. But here and there, when I feel too steeped in feelings that are new for me —feelings like need, like love, like I think I love him. The last time I loved a guy, he trampled on me, killed my spirit, turned me into a kissing machine detached from heart and head and love. Whatever love is.

But that's the thing. I am beginning to know love. Not because I feel it for Joe, but because it's what he shows me. And I am not used to seeing love in someone else: the way he wears it on his chest, in his fingers, in his mouth when he laughs at me, grins at something I say, or kisses the knuckles of my hands and rubs them across my cheek; the way his eyes take me in and then show me an image of myself that is not familiar to me—a loved me. I look at him and see myself loved, and this is scary, pushing me out of his apartment or my apartment or his car and into the clubs, looking for a guy who will kiss the love out of me, remind me that I am not special, just another girl, another available vagina, steeling herself against desire and anything that will put me in danger of losing myself to stirrings I am too scared to face, to give into.

I push him away by kissing a stranger who pretends to love me for the ten minutes we're lip-locked, swearing to myself that Joe is just another Joe who wants what I am not ready to give him. Except he doesn't. He doesn't push me for sex. Doesn't bring it up. He kisses me, touches me only when and where I let him, and doesn't shove his hands all over me like he expects more or is deserved of more.

He feeds me. Not just food. He buys me cards and fills them with fancy scrawlings full of words and kindness that tell me how he feels about me. He tells me what he sees when he looks at me—not sex. Not a mouth and a kiss. Nothing physical. He talks about my tenderness, my goodness, how I surprise him with my intelligence, the way I look out at the world with innocence despite my hardships. I have a box full of cards he's given me, and one day, I go out and buy him one. It's the first one since the card I bought for Sean and then ripped up at the club when I saw him kissing another girl. My card for Joe has a cat hanging from a tree branch. On the inside, it says, "Hang in there," appropriate for his job-hunting endeavors. A few months later, I buy another one and fill it with Alanis Morissette's lyrics from "Head Over Feet."

I take small steps into things. Like dating, loving, and even having sex. Or at least, wanting to. True to his word, Joe has not brought up sex. It hasn't come up. He has his hands full trying to combat all these walls I don't know I have put up—walls that not only keep guys out of my sex but also out of my heart. How could they love me when I haven't been honest with them, have not let them see the girl who breathes and coughs and sighs behind the walls erected between them and me? I am out the door before they can say my name, before sex ever comes up. And I pretend this is okay with me. But now here I am, standing before a boy who wants to know me, plying layer after layer of protective film I have wrapped around me to support my isolation and innocence. It's a big job, but he doesn't complain, doesn't blame me, doesn't get angry as he pulls each layer off with care, quietly assessing what is hidden beneath. Another layer. Another fear. Another lie I have dressed into a pretty little truth with pink ruffles and polka dot bows to hide all the loneliness that swallows in hard gulps beneath, gasping for air, for detection, for relief.

Joe's love is boundless, patient, quiet. He's not ashamed to show me, and he shows it without cheapening it with words—clichéd words like "I love you." These words don't come at me in the months we date, as if he knows that if they do, they will make me run in the opposite direction like a bunny being chased by a feral cat without any hope for survival. This love of his creeps beneath my skin when I'm at the clubs, while I'm flirting with a stupid boy whose name I will forget as soon as I'm in Helen's car, tossing the paper with his number on it out the window, forcing the wind to take it and shred its worthlessness. Everywhere I go, wherever I am, I see him, Joe, paying attention to me, doing things for me, kind things, loving things, and I am torn.

He cooks Chicken Francese for me in his apartment, and I consume the lemon and butter flavor that satiates my senses and the hunger pangs inside my belly that have nothing to do with food. He picks me up from school, so I don't have to wait for the bus at night, in the dead of winter. He surprises me with thermal gloves for the times he can't get to me, and he buys me a winter coat with fur on the inside even though he has about $300 in the bank so I don't have to walk in the cold with my sweatshirts since I don't like to wear coats. He reads my poems, poems no one has ever read, poems about courting death as if he is a great lover who has devoured my entire being, in body and in soul. Joe takes in my darkness and reflects his light, turning me to face the floor-length mirror in his apartment his older sister left behind so I can see what he sees when he looks at me. I avert my face, but when he pushes my chin back to the reflection of him standing behind me, his arms about my waist, his chin resting on my head, I only see him, the love in his eyes that he doesn't hide, and I feel my spine resting into his stomach and chest as if unencumbered for the first time.

He drops by my house in the morning before I go to work with coffee and a buttered bagel in one hand and a radio playing a song from *The Phantom of the Opera*, a musical I dragged him to see when my boss gave us free tickets, in the other. He picks me up from work and drives me to surprise destinations. Once, he takes me to a Bon Jovi concert. Neither one of us can afford to pay for the tickets, so he parks his car at the parking lot at Jones Beach, and with Bon Jovi's voice crooning in the background, Joe whisks a champagne bottle and two plastic cups from the back seat. We toast to us and kiss while mosquitoes nip on the sweet sweat on our arms and legs. He drops off flowers at my house when it is least expected, and on the few occasions I am not home, he actually confronts my mother without fear or hesitation.

"She's a piece of work," he confesses to me after the first time he rings the doorbell to surprise me with flowers.

"Kathryn is not home," she told him, peeking out of the living room window of our apartment on the third floor, about to slide the glass lids closed, ending the conversation.

"Well, can you just take the flowers and give them to her?" he yelled up at her.

"I am in my robe," she offered back, closing the window all the way before he can say anything more.

Joe rang the bell. He rang again. And again. He rang until she slid the window open, tossing a stony expression in his direction below, her lips drawn into a long, tight, inflexible line.

"Would you just take the flowers, please? I don't want to leave them out here. Someone might take them," he smiled up at her, as if her rudeness does not impact him.

She closed the window, he tells me. A few long minutes later, she came down, opened the main door to the building, took the flowers from him, and told him to call before he visits, to make sure I am home, so she doesn't have to answer the door in her robe.

"Sure." He grinned at her, ran to his car, and peeled away.

Whenever he comes to pick me up and she's around, he is polite to her. "Hello, Ann," he tries to lock eyes with her, even though she doesn't respond to him, only casting him an icy glare.

"Are you going out with *him*?" she asks me one day.

Joe is right there, standing beside us. I am showing him the garden beside our building, the garden I spent much of my teen years mowing and weeding just to get out of the house that had begun to feel like a tomb in which my mother and I had been buried alive, staring at each other to see who would run out of air first.

"You mean, Joe? That *him*?" I ask her, embarrassed for Joe. But he just winks at me. I wish I could just roll her rudeness off my shoulders with the ease that he appears to possess. Nothing about my mother fazes him. Her words cut me with razor-sharp precision, leaving behind open, raw, bloodied lines that sting when the air hits them.

"She's just an old lady," he points out when we're in his car. "Old people get crotchety, rude. I'm used it, from my father. He was fun-loving but in his old age, right before he died, he lost his filter. You just have to remind yourself who she is and then not let her bother you. All the stuff she says and does, it's all her. It's about her. It has nothing to do with you."

And then I decide. I decide to tell him.

"My real name is Marina," I blurt while he's driving.

"What?"

"My name. My birth name is Marina. Ann adopted me when I was eight and changed it to Kathryn. That's why I won't let anyone call me Kathryn. It's the name only she calls me. I'm Marina."

"That's a pretty name." He is quiet, as if giving me the space I need to tell him the rest of it.

And so I tell him. I tell him that I was born in Greece. That my birth mother was abusive and beat my father. That he left all of us—my mother, my two brothers, me, and my two sisters. That when he left, she picked up with a man who sold her for money and that we were all placed in orphanages. That my aunt took me and then put me up for adoption. That Ann found out about me and adopted me all the way from Greece. That she loved me as her own until I wouldn't give up my family, their names, my memories. And then she gave up trying to be my mother, reminding me that I come from a whore every time I go out, and she calls me a *putana*, interrogating my body with eyes that strip me, looking for fingerprints on my skin, hickeys on my neck, penetration of my body—just to prove that she is right, that I am a whore. That I am not hers.

Joe pulls over, puts the car in park, and wraps me in his arms.

"Marina." He says my name aloud, filling the spaces around us with the letters and syllables of my silenced childhood. And he doesn't know this, but it is the first time since I was adopted that someone, anyone, has called me by my birth name. His voice is like thick milk draped all over my name, all over me, so smooth and sweet and comforting that I want to sink into it in all my nakedness and weep.

And this is when I know. When I know that I love him. That he is the one.

THE LAST GREEK-
AMERICAN VIRGIN

Joe and I have been dating for a year and a half, but we still have not had sex. For the first time in my life, I want to have sex. With him. We do everything but have sex. We lie naked on his bed, twisting our legs around each other, with tangled sheets between us, all around us. I have experienced all my firsts with him. And even though I won't seal the deal with intercourse, Joe is still patient, still loving, still with me, teaching me all the secrets of lovemaking that I have resisted for so many years. I no longer have to ask my friends what orgasms feel like, or how they can be faked. I don't ever want to fake one, and with Joe, I don't have to. He's attentive, no matter how long it takes me to feel the shudders overtake me and leave me spent and exhausted, wanting so much to take a drag from Joe's cigarette, even though I don't smoke.

"I think it's your mother," he tells me one night, his lips brushing against my belly button. "I think there's a part of you that feels so indebted to her, that wants her approval so much, that you won't let yourself go."

I close my eyes as his lips trail lower, grabbing his hair and pulling gently, arching my back and pushing into his mouth. I don't want to think about my mother. Or the hold she has on me. I only want to surrender to the love my body and I feel from his hands and mouth, planting seeds of pleasure that sprout from the pores on my skin like wildflowers.

"Perhaps," I sigh. Deep down, I know that he is partly right. We have been going out for more than a year, and although we fool around, every time the desire to go all the way grips me, I resist. I tense up. The thing is, I don't think I can have sex until I am out from under the stifling rules of her home, her mothering. I have to free myself from her first and then I can free my inhibitions. When I have sex for the first time, I want it to be for me. I want to feel it all for myself, without her voice searing its way into my thoughts like a sharp knife slicing away the happiness I have found despite all her efforts to destroy it with her forebodings that my actions will result in self-debasement.

My opportunity for escape comes when my mother leaves for a trip to China. No matter how far away she is, however, my mother still has to go on her terms, with certain control mechanisms posited to keep me in line.

"Please do not bring your friend over to this house while I'm away," she locks me into her gaze, her thin lips drawing a line I dare not cross. "I will know."

"Trust me, he doesn't want to come here," I laugh at her self-importance.

"And I don't want you staying at his place, either."

"Sure." I roll my eyes at her. I have never spent a night at Joe's, even making him drive me home in the middle of a blizzard a few months earlier, despite his protests and the two-hour drive on barren, snow-draped roads and blinding winds pounding against us as we crawled through it. Fear always brings me back to her—but that is the only reason I return. It's never out of love or respect.

"When are you returning?" I ask her out of curiosity.

"What, so you can stay over his place? I'm not telling you." She gives me the smug look of one who has all the power, all the information.

"Why? I just want to know when you will come back. How will I know if something goes wrong on your trip? How do I get in touch with you if something happens to me?" All these, I think, are good questions when someone travels to another continent. Especially when that someone is half your family.

"You will just have to find out when I get back."

"Whatever." I wave my hand at her with disgust. "Enjoy your trip." I grab my house keys and leave the house before I say or do anything I will regret, walking down to the park I have used as my refuge from her eyes and tone and face since my middle school years. I find the swings I used to rock me back and forth whenever I want everything around me to be quiet and still, to pretend that I am in the arms of a loving parent rolling love into me one sway at a time. If only I could still all the clamor and rage that live in my thoughts. Although I have limbs that can walk and run away from her, I am paralyzed, and I'm never sure why. When I return home, she is gone.

I keep my promise to her and Joe does not come over, but neither of us wants him to come to this house. This house enfolds me in starkness, in coldness. It has locks on doors and thermostats and phones—all intended to shut me out, to control me, to keep me in line, all designed by a woman with an intricate and invisible lock on her own heart, disabling her from loving freely, without conditions and reproaches.

It never occurs to me to say, "Fuck you and your stupid rules." Fear of displeasing her, fear of losing her, fear of disobeying her still permeates, preventing me from acting autonomously, like an adult. My shackles are strong and secure, as are my apprehensions for growing up and leaving her, alone, without me. Leaving me without her. She is all I have ever known. Her kind of love is all I have known.

Until Joe, that is. He has taught me that love is not about locks and shackles. It's unconditional. It's loving someone with all the ugly and the good. It's an honest love, an open one. So no, I don't want to bring Joe back to my mother's house, a house in which I live as a stranger, a foreign object that does not belong but has nowhere else to go.

I spend all my time in his apartment. And despite the aged appearance of it, the water stains on the bathroom wall, the old and tattered carpet from the 1970s—when his father lived in it —with dog pee stains on it that will never be erased, the tiny kitchen that can only fit one person at a time, I am at home. It is warm, inviting, a place where I can kiss the boy I love without feeling as if every wall is a pair of reproaching eyes denouncing me for my whorishness. Instead, its walls are honey-toned and safe, enveloping me with an ease and acceptance that does not exist in my own home. I fit in here. I belong.

One night, Joe and I meet a few of his friends in the city. We have a great time and a little too much to drink. Too drunk to move, to think or speak, I fall asleep on Joe's bed, fully dressed. I am too drunk to consider my mother's rules and the possibility of her returning from her trip.

Joe wakes me up the next day, drives me to work, picks me up after work, as he often does, takes me to dinner at Uno Pizzeria, and then drops me off in front of my house. My mother has returned from her trip.

"You slept over *his* place," she accuses me, placing forced emphasis on the pronoun that has become a substitute for Joe's name. "I told you not to."

"Yeah, so?" This is my only response to her as I make my way into my messy room.

"Did you have sex with him?" She follows me down the hall.

"That is none of your business. I'm almost twenty-five years old. I don't need to defend myself to you."

"This is my house," she begins.

"Whatever," I interrupt and face her with a look that says, "who cares?"

"You disobeyed me, and I will not have it. If you keep this up then I want you to move out," she threatens me. This threat has kept me in line before, often used to keep me from going out with my friends. But this is the first time I don't feel the anxiety her warning usually engenders. I don't think about how hard it will be to pay for school and rent. Or about the difficulties of surviving on my own—without her as security. I don't consider all the things that can go wrong. Or the guilt of abandoning the woman who saved me by adopting me.

I look at her for a long, quiet moment. My heart is pounding, but I only hear it in the distance, throbbing but muted. Powerless.

"If you kick me out, you won't like where I go," I tell her without thinking. My voice is calm and in control, surprising even me.

"You're going to move in with *him?*" Her words lash out at me, spewed spit caught in the air between us.

"He's been asking me for a while now, and perhaps I should," I say in a nonchalant tone.

She laughs then. A cold and disarming laugh that has observed some irony. "This is what everyone warned me about, you know. No one wanted me to adopt you." She shakes her head at me and laughs again. "My family was against it from the beginning."

"Why?" I ask, feeling like I have been punched in the face. You'd think I would be used to her callousness by now, but I am always unprepared for it.

"Well, my family warned me not to adopt an older child. My cousin said that you would probably come with problems. There was someone in her family who adopted two young girls and they both turned out to be loose girls. They had sex, took drugs, and ran away from home at a young age."

My mother says all this knowingly, as if I should understand the rationale she is sharing with me. As if I have proven her cousin correct in her assumption of adopting someone else's children.

Look at you, I hear her thoughts telling me. *My cousin was right.*

"What does this have to do with me?" I ask.

"Well," she returns in her usual tone of superiority. "I won't tell them that you're living with someone. It's indecent. What will they think?"

"So, you're afraid that your family will say, 'I told you so,' because you adopted me when they advised you against it, and I turned out to be a whore just like those two girls in her family. Just like my birth mother." I point this out with a numb catch in my voice, as if trying to clarify the hidden depths of her fears.

"Yes," is all she says. As if the evidence is wrapped all over me, guilty as charged inscribed on my forehead. "I'm giving you two months then. Move out. Maybe you can move in with your friend Helen," she says. Oh, now she likes Helen. Helen, "the fast one," as she likes to refer to her.

She hasn't heard a word I said. "I don't need two months. I'll be out by the end of the week."

Confidence surges in my veins like new blood transfused as a life-saving force, someone else's blood, someone else's courage coursing through me. Moving in with Joe after a year and a half of dating seems like the next obvious step. I am very comfortable with it, and I smile knowing that everything will be okay. There is nothing for me to fear. Whatever happens in the future, I can take care of myself. Joe has taught me that. He has helped me see that I have the strength and resilience to survive on my own, without her. Even without him, if that is part of my future. My personal freedom is something tangible for the first time, something solid that I can turn over in my fingers and consider as possible, as achievable.

The following weekend, Joe and I move my stuff out of my room, the only space in the apartment that contains evidence of my existence. There is one picture of me in my mother's office—a school picture from the eighth grade—but I don't take that with me. I take only my clothes, my books, my computer, my photo albums, and my cat, Treasure. Those are the only things that belong to me, and I take them with me towards the next phase of my adulthood.

For the first time, I walk away from my mother and into a life without her. My life. A life with many unknowns and in which I make the rules and decisions for my own person, weaving dreams for myself that are not defined by her voice or opinions. A life that will depend solely on me to fulfill it and live it. It feels a lot like a time of renewed hope and celebration.

I long to know myself in the grinning face of freedom, where I can live like a mature woman and make love for the first time without feeling like a whore, a sinful and impotent little girl my mother has fostered, conscious only of the maternal condemnations that stunted her growth.

When I walk through the threshold of Joe's apartment twenty minutes later, I enter as one who lives there—not as the visiting girlfriend. We order pizza and a bottle of Coke and spend the next hour unpacking my boxes, shelving my books, folding my clothes into drawers in furniture already empty and waiting for my things, and introducing my cat to his dog.

When these chores are completed, we fall onto the couch in front of the television set. Joe and I begin to laugh, and I feel light for the first time. Light and unencumbered. What being free feels like.

"I love you, Marina," he says, planting a kiss against my hair. I begin to breathe. Out loud. And I realize that I have been holding my breath all these years. Ever since I lost my name. I curl into the crook of Joe's arm, where I fit perfectly, as if this warm space was made for me, and I know I am home. I am finally loved—the way that I want to be loved—fully and wholly. As me. Not as the girl my mother had tried so hard to mold with the force of steel and fire.

When he kisses me, whispering my name in my ear, I know he is kissing me, Marina—not Kathryn. And I open myself up to him for the first time, shedding the well-worn and guarded remains of my virginity without reservations or guilt, laughing and weeping with the joy of being found.

This is love.

ACKNOWLEDGMENTS

My gratitude primarily goes to my children, Joseph and Marina, for making my writing part of our family discussions and for giving me the time and space needed to be a writer. Without their participation and support, this book would not have been written. It is for them that I write and endeavor to fulfill my dreams, so they can learn to make their own dreams a reality.

Thank you to Brooke Warner and the She Writes staff for offering me a generous contract in publishing my book and making the process so easy and flawless.

Many thanks to my Women's Fiction Writers Association (WFWA) peers, and special gratitude to Michele Montgomery for organizing and sustaining daily writing Zooms during the pandemic. You provided a safe and trusting space for all of us to create and revise as well as console and advise each other. I've never written as much as I have since joining this organization and this virtual writing space. Thank you to all my WFWA sisters for showing up, reading, and supporting this invaluable work we do out of love.

ABOUT THE AUTHOR

Credit: Joseph DelVecchio

Author of the award-winning debut novel, *Dear Jane*, Marina DelVecchio is a college professor and writer who focuses her work on the internal and external struggles of women. Her writing can be found online and in print. Born in Greece and raised in New York, she currently lives with her children in North Carolina.

SELECTED TITLES FROM SHE WRITES PRESS

She Writes Press is an independent publishing company founded to serve women writers everywhere. Visit us at www.shewritespress.com.

Erotic Integrity: How to be True to Yourself Sexually by Claudia Six, PhD. $16.95, 978-1-63152-079-2. Dr. Claudia Six, a respected clinical sexologist and relationship coach, presents her unique method to uncovering your true sexual desires and attaining a more authentic and satisfying sexuality.

Fetish Girl: A Memoir of Sex, Domination, and Motherhood by Bella LaVey. $16.95, 978-1-63152-435-6. A kinky roller coaster ride through addiction, violence, motherhood, sex, and the creation of Evil Kitty, Bella LaVey's larger-than-life dominatrix persona, this singular memoir is the story of a woman attracted to extremes who is willing to go to great lengths to uncover and make peace with her true nature.

First Date Stories: Women's Romantic to Ridiculous Midlife Adventures by Jodi Klein. $16.95, 978-1-64742-185-4. A collection of hopeful, hilarious, and horrific tales—plus dating tips and inspirational quotes—designed to remind women in their mid-thirties and beyond that not all first dates are created equal, and sometimes they can be the beginning of something wonderful.

Daring to Date Again: A Memoir by Ann Anderson Evans. $16.95, 978-1-63152-909-2. A hilarious, no-holds-barred memoir about a legal secretary turned professor who dives back into the dating pool headfirst after twelve years of celibacy.

Not Exactly Love: A Memoir by Betty Hafner. $16.95, 978-1-63152-149-2. At twenty-five, Betty Hafner thought she'd found the man to make her dream of a family and cozy home come true—but after they married, his rages turned the dream into a nightmare, and Betty had to decide: stay with the man she loved, or find a way to leave?